perfect
pasta

Bath New York Singapore Hong Kong Cologne Delhi Melbourne

This edition published by Parragon in 2008

Parragon
Queen Street House
4 Queen Street
Bath BA1 1HE, UK

Copyright © Parragon Books Ltd 2007
Designed by Terry Jeavons & Company

ISBN 978-1-4054-7370-5

Printed in China

Notes for the reader
This book uses imperial, metric, and US cup measurements. Follow the same units of measurement throughout; do not mix imperial and metric. All spoon measurements are level, unless otherwise stated: teaspoons are assumed to be 5ml, and tablespoons are assumed to be 15ml. Unless otherwise stated, milk is assumed to be whole, eggs and individual fruits such as bananas are medium, and pepper is freshly ground black pepper.

Recipes using raw or very lightly cooked eggs should be avoided by infants, the elderly, pregnant women, convalescents, and anyone suffering from an illness. Pregnant and breast-feeding women are advised to avoid eating peanuts and peanut products.

perfect
pasta

introduction

Where would we be without pasta? It has to be the most useful invention ever—it is delicious, inexpensive, nutritious, quick and easy to cook, very satisfying, and incredibly versatile. The fact that it comes in so many shapes and sizes makes it even more interesting, as well as fun to eat for adults and children alike.

The shape you use is largely a matter of choice, and you have about 200 different shapes to choose from! There are, of course, a few classic combinations. Spaghetti, for example, is the one to serve with meatballs or a rich, meaty, bolognese sauce—if you want to be both well fed and entertained, look out for the really long

variety of spaghetti, which is quite a challenge to eat! Macaroni & Cheese simply wouldn't be the same made with any other shape of pasta, and Fettuccine Alfredo has a ring to the name that pasta lovers know well!

Pasta is almost foolproof to cook, but it's worth noting one or two points. Firstly, always bring the cooking water to a rapid boil before adding the pasta. Once the pasta is in the pan, adjust the heat so that the pasta cooks at a steady boil without boiling over. And the most important thing to remember is not to overcook the pasta. 'Al dente' means 'still firm when bitten' and this is what you need to aim for—eating limp, soggy pasta is quite an unpleasant experience! Follow the recommended cooking time in the recipe or on the package and keep tasting toward the end of the time to make sure you get it just right—or you can, of course, follow the Italian tradition of throwing a test piece at the wall and if it sticks, you'll know it's done!

Making your own fresh pasta is surprisingly easy and there are a few recipes for you to try. For everyday use, though, fill your store cupboards with a good variety of pasta shapes, select your favorite dishes, and make the most of this treasure of an ingredient.

soups & salads

Adding pasta to a soup adds an extra texture and 'bite'. Look out for packages of special soup pasta shapes, which are small and cook in almost no time, or use fine vermicelli, broken into pieces. The classic Italian pasta soup is Minestrone, which is packed with vegetables and beans, and is ideal as a substantial lunch or supper dish, served with fresh crusty bread. Brown Lentil & Pasta Soup, Italian Chicken Soup, Fish Soup with Anellini, and Genoese Vegetable Soup are also full of protein and very satisfying. Blending pesto sauce into a soup makes it rich and delicious, or use it as a topping, French-style, in Vegetable & Bean Soup.

Pasta salads are just fabulous, and you can really make the most of all the creative shapes that are available. As the name implies, ear-shaped pasta goes into Orecchietti Salad with Pears & Bleu Cheese, a gorgeous blend of flavors and textures. Pasta Salad with Nuts & Gorgonzola uses farfalle, little bow shapes that go particularly well in salads, and fusilli tricolore—pasta spirals in plain, spinach, and tomato flavors to represent the colors of the Italian flag—goes into Pasta Niçoise, a twist on the classic French salad which looks beautiful and would make a stunning centerpiece for an alfresco summer lunch. It tastes quite wonderful, too!

minestrone

ingredients

SERVES 6

2 tbsp olive oil

2 oz/55 g rindless pancetta or
   lean bacon, diced

2 onions, sliced

2 garlic cloves, finely chopped

3 carrots, chopped

2 celery stalks, chopped

8 oz/225 g/1 cup dried
   cannellini beans, soaked
   overnight in cold water
   to cover

14 oz/400 g canned chopped
   tomatoes

64 fl oz/2 liters/8 cups beef
   stock

12 oz/350 g potatoes, diced

6 oz/175 g dried pepe
   bucato, macaroni, or
   other soup pasta shapes

6 oz/175 g green beans, sliced

4 oz/115 g/1 cup fresh or
   frozen peas

8 oz/225 g savoy cabbage,
   shredded

3 tbsp chopped fresh flat-leaf
   parsley

salt and pepper

fresh Parmesan cheese
   shavings, to serve

method

1 Heat the olive oil in a large, heavy-bottom pan. Add the pancetta, onions, and garlic and cook, stirring occasionally, for 5 minutes.

2 Add the carrots and celery and cook, stirring occasionally, for an additional 5 minutes, or until all the vegetables are softened.

3 Drain the soaked beans and add them to the pan with the tomatoes and their can juices and the beef stock. Bring to a boil, then reduce the heat, cover, and let simmer for 1 hour.

4 Add the potatoes, re-cover, and cook for 15 minutes, then add the pasta, green beans, peas, cabbage, and parsley. Cover and cook for an additional 15 minutes, or until all the vegetables are tender. Season with salt and pepper. Ladle the soup into warmed soup bowls and serve immediately with Parmesan cheese shavings.

potato & pesto soup

ingredients

SERVES 4

3 strips rindless, smoked,
    fatty bacon or pancetta
1 lb/450 g mealy potatoes
1 lb/450 g onions
2 tbsp olive oil
20 fl oz/625 ml/2^1/$_2$ cups
    chicken stock
20 fl oz/625 ml/2^1/$_2$ cups milk
3^1/$_2$ oz/100 g dried conchigliette
5 fl oz/150 ml/^{2}/$_3$ cup heavy
    cream
chopped fresh parsley
salt and pepper
garlic bread and Parmesan
    cheese shavings, to serve

pesto sauce

2 oz/55 g finely chopped
    fresh parsley
2 garlic cloves, crushed
2 oz/55 g/^{1}/$_2$ cup pine nuts,
    crushed
2 tbsp chopped fresh basil
    leaves
2 oz/55 g/^{1}/$_2$ cup freshly
    grated Parmesan cheese
white pepper
5 fl oz/150 ml/^{2}/$_3$ cup olive oil

method

1 To make the pesto sauce, put all of the ingredients in a blender or food processor and process for 2 minutes, or blend by hand using a mortar and pestle.

2 Finely chop the bacon, potatoes, and onions. Cook the bacon in a large pan over medium heat for 4 minutes. Add the oil, potatoes, and onions, and cook for 12 minutes, stirring constantly.

3 Add the stock and milk to the pan, bring to a boil and let simmer for 10 minutes. Add the conchigliette and let simmer for an additional 10–12 minutes.

4 Blend in the cream and let simmer for 5 minutes. Add the chopped parsley, salt and pepper, and 2 tablespoons of the pesto sauce. Transfer the soup to individual serving bowls and serve with Parmesan cheese shavings and fresh garlic bread.

fresh tomato soup

ingredients

SERVES 4

1 tbsp olive oil

1 lb 7 oz/650 g plum
   tomatoes

1 onion, cut into fourths

1 garlic clove, sliced thinly

1 celery stalk, chopped
   coarsely

18 fl oz/500 ml/generous
   2 cups chicken stock

2 oz/55 g/$^1/_2$ cup dried anellini
   or other soup pasta

salt and pepper

fresh flat-leaf parsley,
   chopped, to garnish

method

1 Pour the olive oil into a large, heavy-bottom pan and add the tomatoes, onion, garlic, and celery. Cover and cook over low heat for 45 minutes, occasionally shaking the pan gently, until the mixture is pulpy.

2 Transfer the mixture to a food processor or blender and process to a smooth purée. Push the purée through a strainer into a clean pan.

3 Add the stock and bring to a boil. Add the pasta, bring back to a boil, and cook for 8–10 minutes, until the pasta is tender but still firm to the bite. Season with salt and pepper. Ladle into warmed bowls, sprinkle with the parsley, and serve immediately.

brown lentil & pasta soup

ingredients

SERVES 4

4 strips lean bacon, cut into
   small squares
1 onion, chopped
2 garlic cloves, crushed
2 celery stalks, chopped
1³/₄ oz/50 g farfalline or
   spaghetti, broken into
   small pieces
14 oz/400 g canned brown
   lentils, drained
40 fl oz/1.25 liters/5 cups hot
   vegetable stock
2 tbsp chopped fresh mint
fresh mint sprigs, to garnish

method

1 Place the bacon in a large skillet together with the onion, garlic, and celery. Dry fry for 4–5 minutes, stirring, until the onion is tender and the bacon is just beginning to brown.

2 Add the pasta to the skillet and cook, stirring, for 1 minute to coat the pasta in the fat.

3 Add the lentils and the stock, and bring to a boil. Reduce the heat and let simmer for 12–15 minutes, or until the pasta is tender but still firm to the bite.

4 Remove the skillet from the heat and stir in the chopped fresh mint. Transfer the soup to warmed soup bowls, garnish with fresh mint sprigs, and serve immediately.

italian chicken soup

ingredients

SERVES 4

1 lb/450 g skinless, boneless
   chicken breast, cut into
   thin strips
40 fl oz/1.25 liters/5 cups
   chicken stock
5 fl oz/150 ml/^{2}/$_3$ cup heavy
   cream
4 oz/115 g dried vermicelli
salt and pepper
1 tbsp cornstarch
3 tbsp milk
6 oz/175 g canned corn
   kernels, drained

method

1 Place the chicken in a large pan and pour in the chicken stock and cream. Bring to a boil, then reduce the heat and let simmer for 20 minutes.

2 Meanwhile, bring a large heavy-bottom pan of lightly salted water to a boil. Add the pasta, return to a boil, and cook for 10–12 minutes, or until just tender but still firm to the bite. Drain the pasta well and keep warm.

3 Season the soup with salt and pepper. Mix the cornstarch and milk together until a smooth paste forms, then stir it into the soup. Add the corn and pasta and heat through. Ladle the soup into warmed soup bowls and serve.

chicken & pasta broth

ingredients

SERVES 6

12 oz/350 g boneless
    chicken breasts
2 tbsp corn oil
1 onion, diced
9 oz/250 g/2 cups carrots,
    diced
9 oz/250 g cauliflower florets
28 fl oz/940 ml/3^1/$_2$ cups
    chicken stock
2 tsp dried mixed herbs
4^1/$_2$ oz/125 g dried small
    pasta shapes
salt and pepper
freshly grated Parmesan
    cheese, for sprinkling
    (optional)
fresh crusty bread, to serve

method

1 Using a sharp knife, finely dice the chicken, discarding any skin.

2 Heat the corn oil in a large pan and quickly cook the chicken, onion, carrots, and cauliflower until they are lightly colored.

3 Stir in the chicken stock and dried mixed herbs, and bring to a boil.

4 Add the pasta shapes to the pan and return to a boil. Cover the pan and let the broth simmer for 10 minutes, stirring occasionally to prevent the pasta sticking together.

5 Season the broth with salt and pepper and sprinkle with grated Parmesan cheese, if using. Serve with crusty bread.

fish soup with anellini

ingredients

SERVES 6

2 tbsp olive oil

2 onions, sliced

1 garlic clove, finely chopped

32 fl oz/1 liter/4 cups
   fish stock or water

14 oz/400 g canned chopped
   tomatoes

1/4 tsp herbes de Provence

1/4 tsp saffron threads

4 oz/115 g dried anellini

salt and pepper

1 lb/450 g monkfish fillet, cut
   into chunks

18 live mussels, scrubbed
   and debearded*

8 oz/225 g raw shrimp, shelled
   and deveined, tails left on

* discard any damaged
mussels or any that do
not shut immediately
when tapped

method

1 Heat the olive oil in a large heavy-bottom pan. Add the onions and garlic and cook over low heat, stirring occasionally, for 5 minutes, or until the onions have softened.

2 Add the fish stock with the tomatoes and their can juices, herbs, saffron, and pasta, and season with salt and pepper. Bring to a boil, then cover and let simmer for 15 minutes.

3 Add the fish, mussels, and shrimp. Re-cover the pan and let simmer for an additional 5–10 minutes, until the mussels have opened, the shrimp have changed color, and the fish is opaque and flakes easily. Discard any mussels that remain closed. Ladle the soup into warmed bowls and serve.

white bean soup

ingredients

SERVES 4

6 oz/175 g/³/₄ cup dried
  cannellini beans, soaked
  overnight in cold water
  to cover
48 fl oz/1.6 liters/6 cups
  chicken or vegetable stock
4 oz/115 g dried spirali
6 tbsp olive oil
2 garlic cloves, finely chopped
4 tbsp chopped fresh flat-leaf
  parsley
salt and pepper
fresh crusty bread, to serve

method

1 Drain the soaked beans and place them in a large, heavy-bottom pan. Add the stock and bring to a boil. Partially cover the pan, reduce the heat, and let simmer for 2 hours, or until tender.

2 Transfer about half the beans and a little of the stock to a food processor or blender and process to a smooth purée. Return the purée to the pan and stir well to mix. Return the soup to a boil.

3 Add the pasta to the soup, return to a boil, and cook for 10 minutes, or until tender.

4 Meanwhile, heat 4 tablespoons of the olive oil in a small pan. Add the garlic and cook over low heat, stirring frequently, for 4–5 minutes, or until golden. Stir the garlic into the soup and add the parsley. Season with salt and pepper and ladle into warmed soup bowls. Drizzle with the remaining olive oil and serve immediately with crusty bread.

genoese vegetable soup

ingredients

SERVES 8

7 oz/200 g spinach leaves

8 oz/225 g plum tomatoes

2 onions, sliced

2 carrots, diced

2 celery stalks, sliced

2 potatoes, diced

4 oz/115 g/1 cup frozen peas

4 oz/115 g green beans, cut
into 1-inch/2.5-cm lengths

2 zucchini, diced

3 garlic cloves, sliced

4 tbsp olive oil

48 fl oz/2 liters/8 cups
vegetable or chicken stock

salt and pepper

5 oz/140 g dried soup pasta

freshly grated Parmesan
cheese, to serve

pesto sauce

2 garlic cloves

1 oz/25 g/$^1/_4$ cup pine nuts

4 oz/115 g fresh basil leaves

salt

2 oz/55 g/$^1/_2$ cup freshly
grated Parmesan cheese

4 fl oz/125 ml/$^1/_2$ cup olive oil

method

1 Remove any coarse stalks from the spinach and shred. Peel the tomatoes by cutting a cross in the bottom of each and placing in a heatproof bowl. Cover with boiling water and let stand for 35–45 seconds. Drain and plunge into cold water, then peel. Seed and dice the tomatoes, then place in a large, heavy-bottom pan together with the onions, carrots, celery, potatoes, peas, beans, zucchini, and garlic. Pour in the olive oil and stock and bring to a boil over medium-low heat. Reduce the heat and let simmer gently for about 1$^1/_2$ hours.

2 Meanwhile, make the pesto. Put the garlic, pine nuts, basil, and a pinch of salt into a mortar and pound to a paste with a pestle. Transfer the mixture to a bowl and gradually work in the Parmesan cheese, using a wooden spoon, followed by the olive oil, to make a thick, creamy sauce. Taste and adjust the seasoning if necessary. Cover with plastic wrap and let chill in the refrigerator until required.

3 Season the soup and add the pasta. Cook for an additional 8–10 minutes, or until the pasta is tender but still firm to the bite. Stir in half the pesto, remove the pan from the heat, and let stand for 4 minutes. Taste and add more salt, pepper, and pesto if necessary. Ladle into warmed bowls and serve at once. Hand round the freshly grated Parmesan cheese separately.

vegetable & bean soup

ingredients

SERVES 4–6

8 oz/225 g fresh fava beans

2 tbsp olive oil

2 large garlic cloves, crushed

1 large onion, finely chopped

1 celery stalk, finely chopped

1 carrot, peeled and chopped

6 oz/175 g firm new
    potatoes, diced

30 fl oz/940 ml/3³/₄ cups
    vegetable stock

2 beefsteak tomatoes, peeled,
    seeded, and chopped

salt and pepper

1 large bunch of fresh basil,
    tied with kitchen string

7 oz/200 g zucchini, diced

7 oz/200 g green beans,
    trimmed and chopped

2 oz/55 g dried vermicelli,
    broken into pieces, or
    small pasta shapes

pesto sauce

3¹/₂ oz/100 g fresh basil leaves

2 large garlic cloves

1¹/₂ tbsp pine nuts

2 fl oz/50 ml/scant ¹/₄ cup
    fruity extra-virgin olive oil

2 oz/55 g/¹/₂ cup finely grated
    Parmesan cheese

method

1 If the fava beans are very young and tender, they can be used as they are. If they are older, use a small, sharp knife to slit the gray outer skins, then 'pop' out the green beans.

2 Heat the olive oil in a large heavy-bottom pan, over medium heat. Add the garlic, onion, celery, and carrot and sauté until the onion is soft, but not brown.

3 Add the potatoes, stock, and tomatoes, and season with salt and pepper. Bring the stock to a boil, skimming the surface if necessary, then add the basil. Reduce the heat and cover the pan. Let simmer for 15 minutes, or until the potatoes are tender.

4 Meanwhile, make the pesto sauce. Whiz the basil, garlic, and pine nuts in a food processor or blender until a thick paste forms. Add the extra-virgin olive oil and whiz again. Transfer to a bowl and stir in the cheese, then cover and chill until required.

5 When the potatoes are tender, stir the fava beans, zucchini, green beans, and vermicelli into the soup and continue simmering for 10 minutes, or until the vegetables are tender and the pasta is cooked. Taste, and adjust the seasoning if necessary. Remove and discard the bunch of basil.

6 Ladle the soup into bowls and add a spoonful of pesto sauce to each bowl.

pasta niçoise

ingredients

SERVES 4

4 oz/115 g green beans, cut
  into 2-inch/5-cm lengths
8 oz/225 g dried fusilli tricolore
3^1/$_2$ fl oz/100 ml/generous
  ^{1}/$_3$ cup olive oil
2 tuna steaks, about
  12 oz/350 g each
salt and pepper
6 cherry tomatoes, halved
2 oz/55 g/^{1}/$_3$ cup black olives,
  pitted and halved
6 canned anchovies,
  drained and chopped
3 tbsp chopped fresh flat-leaf
  parsley
2 tbsp lemon juice
8–10 radicchio leaves

method

1 Bring a large, heavy-bottom pan of lightly salted water to a boil. Add the green beans, reduce the heat, and cook for 5–6 minutes. Remove with a slotted spoon and refresh in a bowl of cold water. Drain well. Add the pasta to the same pan, return to a boil, and cook for 8–10 minutes, or until tender but still firm to the bite.

2 Meanwhile, brush a grill pan with some of the olive oil and heat until smoking. Season the tuna with salt and pepper and brush both sides with some of the remaining olive oil. Cook over medium heat for 2 minutes on each side, or until cooked to your liking, then remove from the grill pan and reserve.

3 Drain the pasta well and tip it into a bowl. Add the green beans, cherry tomatoes, olives, anchovies, parsley, lemon juice, and remaining olive oil and season with salt and pepper. Toss well and let cool. Remove and discard any skin from the tuna and slice thickly.

4 Gently mix the tuna into the pasta salad. Line a large salad bowl with the radicchio leaves, spoon in the salad, and serve.

tuna & herbed fusilli salad

ingredients

SERVES 4

7 oz/200 g dried fusilli

1 red bell pepper, seeded
   and cut into quarters

5$^{1}/_{2}$ oz/150 g asparagus spears

1 red onion, sliced

4 tomatoes, sliced

7 oz/200 g canned tuna in
   brine, drained and flaked

dressing

6 tbsp basil-flavored oil or
   extra-virgin olive oil

3 tbsp white wine vinegar

1 tbsp lime juice

1 tsp mustard

1 tsp honey

4 tbsp chopped fresh basil,
   plus extra sprigs to garnish

method

1 Bring a large pan of lightly salted water to a boil. Add the pasta, return to a boil, and cook for 8–10 minutes until tender but still firm to the bite.

2 Meanwhile, put the bell pepper quarters under a preheated hot broiler and cook for 10–12 minutes until the skins begin to blacken. Transfer to a plastic bag, seal, and set aside.

3 Bring a separate pan of water to a boil, add the asparagus, and blanch for 4 minutes. Drain and plunge into cold water, then drain again. Remove the pasta from the heat, drain, and set aside to cool. Remove the bell pepper quarters from the bag and peel off the skins. Slice the bell pepper into strips.

4 To make the dressing, put all the dressing ingredients in a large bowl and stir together well. Add the pasta, bell pepper strips, asparagus, onion, tomatoes, and tuna. Toss together gently, then divide among serving bowls. Garnish with basil sprigs and serve.

orecchiette salad with pears & bleu cheese

ingredients

SERVES 4

9 oz/250 g dried orecchiette

1 head of radicchio,
　torn into pieces

1 oak leaf lettuce,
　torn into pieces

2 pears

3 tbsp lemon juice

9 oz/250 g bleu cheese,
　diced

2 oz/55 g/scant 1/2 cup
　chopped walnuts

4 tomatoes, cut into fourths

1 red onion, sliced

1 carrot, grated

8 fresh basil leaves

2 oz/55 g corn salad

4 tbsp olive oil

3 tbsp white wine vinegar

salt and pepper

method

1 Bring a large heavy-bottom pan of lightly salted water to a boil. Add the pasta, return to a boil, and cook for 8–10 minutes, or until tender but still firm to the bite. Drain, refresh in a bowl of cold water and drain again.

2 Place the radicchio and oak leaf lettuce leaves in a large bowl. Halve the pears, remove the cores, and dice the flesh. Toss the diced pear with 1 tablespoon of lemon juice in a small bowl to prevent discoloration. Top the salad with the bleu cheese, walnuts, pears, pasta, tomatoes, onion slices, and grated carrot. Add the basil and corn salad.

3 Mix the remaining lemon juice and the olive oil and vinegar together in a measuring cup, then season with salt and pepper. Pour the dressing over the salad, toss, and serve immediately.

warm pasta salad

ingredients

SERVES 4

8 oz/225 g dried farfalle or
   other pasta shapes
6 pieces of sun-dried tomato
   in oil, drained and chopped
4 scallions, chopped
2 oz/55 g arugula, shredded
1/2 cucumber, seeded
   and diced
salt and pepper
2 tbsp freshly grated
   Parmesan cheese

dressing

4 tbsp olive oil
1/2 tsp superfine sugar
1 tbsp white wine vinegar
1 tsp Dijon mustard
salt and pepper
4 fresh basil leaves,
   finely shredded

method

1 To make the dressing, whisk the olive oil, sugar, vinegar, and mustard together in a bowl. Season with salt and pepper, then stir in the basil.

2 Bring a large, heavy-bottom pan of lightly salted water to a boil. Add the pasta, return to a boil, and cook for 8–10 minutes, or until tender but still firm to the bite. Drain and transfer to a salad bowl. Add the dressing and toss well.

3 Add the chopped sun-dried tomatoes, scallions, arugula, and cucumber, season with salt and pepper, and toss. Sprinkle with the Parmesan cheese and serve warm.

italian salad

ingredients

SERVES 4

8 oz/225 g dried conchiglie

$1^3/_4$ oz/50 g/$^1/_3$ cup pine nuts

12 oz/350 g cherry tomatoes,
    halved

1 red bell pepper, seeded and
    cut into bite-size chunks

1 red onion, chopped

7 oz/200 g mozzarella di
    bufala, cut into small pieces

12 black olives, pitted

1 oz/25 g fresh basil leaves

fresh Parmesan cheese
    shavings, to garnish

dressing

5 tbsp extra-virgin olive oil

2 tbsp balsamic vinegar

1 tbsp chopped fresh basil

salt and pepper

method

1 Bring a large pan of lightly salted water to a boil. Add the pasta, return to a boil, and cook for 8–10 minutes until tender but still firm to the bite. Drain, refresh under cold running water, and drain again. Let cool.

2 Meanwhile, heat a dry skillet over low heat, add the pine nuts, and cook, shaking the skillet frequently, for 1–2 minutes until lightly toasted. Remove from the heat, transfer to a dish, and let cool.

3 To make the dressing, put all the ingredients in a small bowl and mix well together. Cover with plastic wrap, and set aside.

4 To assemble the salad, divide the pasta among 4 serving bowls. Add the pine nuts, tomatoes, bell pepper, onion, cheese, and olives. Sprinkle over the basil, then drizzle over the dressing. Garnish with Parmesan cheese shavings and serve.

pasta salad with curry dressing

ingredients

SERVES 4

4 oz/115 g dried farfalle

4–5 large lettuce leaves

1 green bell pepper, seeded
    and chopped

1 red bell pepper, seeded
    and chopped

2 tbsp chopped fresh chives

4 oz/115 g white mushrooms,
    chopped

dressing

2 tsp curry powder

1 tbsp superfine sugar

4 fl oz/125 ml/$\frac{1}{2}$ cup corn oil

2 fl oz/50 ml/$\frac{1}{4}$ cup white
    wine vinegar

1 tbsp light cream

method

1 Bring a large heavy-bottom pan of lightly salted water to a boil. Add the pasta, return to a boil, and cook for 8–10 minutes, or until tender but still firm to the bite. Drain, rinse in a bowl of cold water, and drain again.

2 Line a large bowl with the lettuce leaves and tip in the pasta. Add the green and red bell peppers, chives, and mushrooms.

3 To make the dressing, place the curry powder and sugar in a small bowl and gradually stir in the oil, vinegar, and cream. Whisk well and pour the dressing over the salad. Toss and serve.

pasta salad with nuts & gorgonzola

ingredients

SERVES 4

8 oz/225 g dried farfalle

2 tbsp walnut oil

4 tbsp safflower oil

2 tbsp balsamic vinegar

salt and pepper

10 oz/280 g mixed salad greens

8 oz/225 g Gorgonzola
    cheese, diced

4 oz/115 g/$\frac{1}{2}$ cup walnuts,
    halved and toasted

method

1 Bring a large heavy-bottom pan of lightly salted water to a boil. Add the pasta, return to a boil, and cook for 8–10 minutes, or until tender but still firm to the bite. Drain and refresh in a bowl of cold water. Drain again.

2 Mix the walnut oil, safflower oil, and vinegar together in a measuring cup, whisking well, and season with salt and pepper.

3 Arrange the salad greens in a large serving bowl. Top with the pasta, Gorgonzola cheese, and walnuts. Pour the dressing over the salad, toss lightly, and serve.

pasta salad with charbroiled bell peppers

ingredients

SERVES 4

1 red bell pepper

1 orange bell pepper

10 oz/280 g dried conchiglie

5 tbsp extra-virgin olive oil

2 tbsp lemon juice

2 tbsp green pesto

1 garlic clove, finely chopped

3 tbsp shredded fresh
     basil leaves

salt and pepper

method

1 Preheat the broiler. Put the whole bell peppers on a cookie sheet and place under the hot broiler, turning frequently, for 15 minutes, or until charred all over. Remove with tongs and place in a bowl. Cover with crumpled paper towels and reserve.

2 Meanwhile, bring a large pan of lightly salted water to a boil. Add the pasta, return to a boil, and cook for 8–10 minutes, or until tender but still firm to the bite.

3 Combine the olive oil, lemon juice, pesto, and garlic in a bowl, whisking well to mix. Drain the pasta, add it to the pesto mixture while still hot, and toss well. Set aside until required.

4 When the bell peppers are cool enough to handle, peel off the skins, then cut open and remove the seeds. Chop the flesh coarsely and add to the pasta with the basil. Season with salt and pepper and toss well. Serve.

meat & poultry

Pasta is useful for making a little meat go a long way! There are some truly delectable meat-based pasta sauces in this section. All devotees of Italian food love Spaghetti & Meatballs, and there is also a recipe for a rather sophisticated Spaghetti Bolognese, another all-time favorite. Two simple yet elegant recipes to try are Spaghetti alla Carbonara and Saffron Linguine—they are both ready to serve in less than fifteen minutes and are dishes to impress guests when you're short of time but big on style. Pasta & Pork in Red Wine Sauce is also very chic, garnished with quail eggs.

If you like a little heat in your pasta sauce, there are plenty of spicy options, including Chile Pork with Tagliatelle, Rigatoni with Ham, Tomato & Chile Sauce, and Macaroni with Sausage, Pepperoncini & Olives. Spaghetti with Parsley Chicken has a delicious, fresh-tasting sauce with lemon zest and a little fresh gingerroot.

If you are keen to have a go at making your own pasta, try Creamy Chicken Ravioli and Chicken Tortellini. Ravioli is very easy, just a matter of spacing out the filling evenly on a sheet of pasta, covering it with a second sheet, and cutting out the squares. Tortellini, on the other hand, involves some manual dexterity, but it's great fun to make and once you've mastered it, you will never look back!

spaghetti & meatballs

ingredients

SERVES 2

2 thick slices white bread,
    crusts removed

2 tbsp olive oil

1 red onion, chopped

2 garlic cloves, finely chopped

14 oz/400 g canned chopped
    tomatoes

8 basil leaves

2 tbsp tomato paste

1 tsp sugar

salt and pepper

1 lb/450 g ground beef

2 eggs

1 tbsp chopped fresh parsley

1 tbsp chopped fresh basil

12 oz/350 g dried spaghetti

freshly grated Parmesan
    cheese, to serve

method

1 Place the bread in a shallow bowl and add just enough water to cover. Soak for 5 minutes, then drain and squeeze the bread to remove all the liquid.

2 Heat the oil in a pan, add the onion and half the garlic, and cook over medium heat, stirring occasionally, for 5 minutes. Add the tomatoes with their juice, basil leaves, tomato paste, and sugar and season with salt and pepper. Bring to a boil, reduce the heat, and let simmer, stirring occasionally, for 20 minutes until thickened and pulpy.

3 Mix the bread, beef, eggs, remaining herbs, garlic, and $1/2$ tsp of salt by hand in a large mixing bowl. Roll small pieces of the meat mixture into balls. Drop the meatballs into the tomato sauce, cover the pan, and cook over medium heat for 30 minutes.

4 Meanwhile, cook the spaghetti in a pan of lightly salted boiling water for 10 minutes, or until tender but still firm to the bite. Drain well.

5 Transfer the spaghetti to a large shallow serving bowl. Arrange the meatballs and sauce on top. Sprinkle 2 tablespoons of freshly grated Parmesan cheese over the top and serve with more cheese in a bowl on the side.

spaghetti bolognese

ingredients

SERVES 4

2 tbsp olive oil

1 tbsp butter

1 small onion, finely chopped

1 carrot, finely chopped

1 celery stalk, finely chopped

$1^3/_4$ oz/50 g mushrooms, diced

8 oz/225 g ground beef

$2^3/_4$ oz/75 g unsmoked bacon
   or ham, diced

2 chicken livers, chopped

2 tbsp tomato paste

4 fl oz/125 ml/$^1/_2$ cup dry
   white wine

salt and pepper

$^1/_2$ tsp freshly grated nutmeg

10 fl oz/300 ml/$1^1/_4$ cups
   chicken stock

4 fl oz/125 ml/$^1/_2$ cup heavy
   cream

1 lb/450 g dried spaghetti

2 tbsp chopped fresh flat-leaf
   parsley, to garnish

freshly grated Parmesan
   cheese, to serve

method

1 Heat the olive oil and butter in a large pan over medium heat. Add the onion, carrot, celery, and mushrooms to the pan, then cook until soft. Add the beef and bacon and cook until the beef is evenly browned.

2 Stir in the chicken livers and tomato paste and cook for 2–3 minutes. Pour in the wine and season with salt, pepper, and the nutmeg. Add the stock. Bring to a boil, then cover and let simmer gently over low heat for 1 hour. Stir in the cream and simmer, uncovered, until reduced.

3 Bring a large pan of lightly salted water to a boil. Add the pasta, return to a boil, and cook until tender but still firm to the bite. Drain and transfer to a warmed serving dish.

4 Spoon the sauce over the pasta, garnish with parsley, and serve with Parmesan cheese.

tagliatelle with a rich meat sauce

ingredients

SERVES 4

4 tbsp olive oil, plus extra
    for serving
3 oz/85 g pancetta or rindless
    lean bacon, diced
1 onion, chopped
1 garlic clove, chopped finely
1 carrot, chopped
1 celery stalk, chopped
8 oz/225 g/1 cup ground
    steak
4 oz/115 g chicken livers,
    chopped
2 tbsp strained tomatoes
4 fl oz/125 ml/$\frac{1}{2}$ cup dry
    white wine
8 fl oz/250 ml/1 cup beef
    stock or water
1 tbsp chopped fresh oregano
1 bay leaf
salt and pepper
1 lb/450 g dried tagliatelle
freshly grated Parmesan
    cheese, to serve

method

1 Heat the olive oil in a large, heavy-bottom pan. Add the pancetta or bacon and cook over medium heat, stirring occasionally, for 3–5 minutes, until it is just turning brown. Add the onion, garlic, carrot, and celery and cook, stirring occasionally, for an additional 5 minutes.

2 Add the steak and cook over high heat, breaking up the meat with a wooden spoon, for 5 minutes, until browned. Stir in the chicken livers and cook, stirring occasionally, for an additional 2–3 minutes. Add the strained tomatoes, wine, stock, oregano, and bay leaf, and season with salt and pepper. Bring to a boil, reduce the heat, cover, and let simmer for 30–35 minutes.

3 When the sauce is almost cooked, bring a large pan of lightly salted water to a boil. Add the pasta, bring back to a boil, and cook for 8–10 minutes, until tender but still firm to the bite. Drain, transfer to a warmed serving dish, drizzle with a little olive oil, and toss well.

4 Remove and discard the bay leaf from the sauce, then pour the sauce over the pasta, toss again, and serve immediately with grated Parmesan cheese.

pasta & pork in red wine sauce

ingredients

SERVES 4

1 lb/450 g pork fillet,
   thinly sliced
4 tbsp olive oil
8 oz/225 g white mushrooms,
   sliced
1 tbsp lemon juice
pinch of saffron threads
12 oz/350 g dried orecchioni
4 tbsp heavy cream
12 quail eggs

red wine sauce

1 tbsp olive oil
1 onion, chopped
1 tbsp tomato paste
7 fl oz/200 ml/³/₄ cup
   red wine
1 tsp oregano, finely chopped

method

1 To make the red wine sauce, heat the oil in a small heavy-bottom pan, add the chopped onion, and cook until transparent. Stir in the tomato paste, red wine, and oregano. Heat gently to reduce and set aside.

2 Pound the slices of pork between 2 sheets of plastic wrap until wafer thin, then cut into strips. Heat the oil in a skillet, add the pork, and stir-fry for 5 minutes. Add the mushrooms to the skillet and stir-fry for an additional 2 minutes. Strain and pour over the red wine sauce. Reduce the heat and let simmer for 20 minutes.

3 Meanwhile, bring a large heavy-bottom pan of lightly salted water to a boil. Add the lemon juice, saffron, and orecchioni, return to a boil and cook for 8–10 minutes, or until tender but still firm to the bite. Drain the pasta thoroughly, return to the pan, and keep warm.

4 Stir the cream into the pan with the pork and heat for a few minutes.

5 Boil the quail eggs for 3 minutes, cool them in cold water and remove the shells. Transfer the pasta to a large, warmed serving plate, top with the pork and the sauce, and garnish with the eggs. Serve immediately.

chile pork with tagliatelle

ingredients

SERVES 4

1 lb/450 g dried tagliatelle

3 tbsp peanut oil

12 oz/350 g pork fillet,
    cut into thin strips

1 garlic clove, finely chopped

1 bunch of scallions, sliced

1-inch/2.5-cm piece fresh
    gingerroot, grated

2 fresh Thai chiles, seeded
    and finely chopped

1 red bell pepper, seeded
    and cut into thin sticks

1 yellow bell pepper, seeded
    and cut into thin sticks

3 zucchini, cut into thin sticks

2 tbsp finely chopped peanuts

1 tsp ground cinnamon

1 tbsp oyster sauce

2 oz/55 g creamed coconut,
    grated

salt and pepper

2 tbsp chopped fresh cilantro,
    to garnish

method

1 Bring a large heavy-bottom pan of lightly salted water to a boil. Add the pasta, return to a boil, and cook for 8–10 minutes, or until tender but still firm to the bite.

2 Meanwhile, heat the peanut oil in a preheated wok or large heavy-bottom skillet. Add the pork and stir-fry for 5 minutes. Add the garlic, scallions, gingerroot, and Thai chiles, and stir-fry for 2 minutes.

3 Add the red and yellow bell peppers and the zucchini and stir-fry for 1 minute. Add the peanuts, cinnamon, oyster sauce, and creamed coconut, and stir-fry for an additional 1 minute. Season with salt and pepper. Drain the pasta and transfer to a serving dish. Top with the chile pork, sprinkle with the chopped cilantro, and serve.

spaghetti alla carbonara

ingredients

SERVES 4

1 lb/450 g dried spaghetti

1 tbsp olive oil

8 oz/225 g rindless pancetta
　　or lean bacon, chopped

4 eggs

5 tbsp light cream

salt and pepper

4 tbsp freshly grated
　　Parmesan cheese

method

1 Bring a large, heavy-bottom pan of lightly salted water to a boil. Add the pasta, return to a boil, and cook for 8–10 minutes, or until tender but still firm to the bite.

2 Meanwhile, heat the olive oil in a heavy-bottom skillet. Add the chopped pancetta and cook over medium heat, stirring frequently, for 8–10 minutes.

3 Beat the eggs with the cream in a small bowl and season with salt and pepper. Drain the pasta and return it to the pan. Tip in the contents of the skillet, then add the egg mixture and half the Parmesan cheese. Stir well, then transfer to a warmed serving dish. Serve immediately, sprinkled with the remaining Parmesan cheese.

rigatoni with spicy bacon & tomato sauce

ingredients

SERVES 4

6 tbsp olive oil

3 garlic cloves, sliced thinly

2³/₄ oz/75 g bacon, chopped

1 lb 12 oz/800 g canned
   chopped tomatoes

¹/₂ tsp dried chile flakes

salt and pepper

1 lb/450 g rigatoni

10 fresh basil leaves, shredded

2 tbsp freshly grated romano
   cheese

method

1 Heat the oil and garlic in a large skillet over medium-low heat. Cook until the garlic is just beginning to color. Add the bacon and cook until browned.

2 Stir in the tomatoes and chile flakes. Season with a little salt and pepper. Bring to a boil, then let simmer over medium-low heat for 30–40 minutes, until the oil separates from the tomatoes.

3 Cook the pasta in plenty of boiling salted water until tender but still firm to the bite. Drain and transfer to a warmed serving dish.

4 Pour the sauce over the pasta. Add the shredded basil and grated romano, then toss well to mix. Serve at once.

linguine with bacon & olives

ingredients

SERVES 4

3 tbsp olive oil

2 onions, thinly sliced

2 garlic cloves, finely chopped

6 oz/175 g rindless lean
    bacon, diced

8 oz/225 g mushrooms, sliced

5 canned anchovy fillets,
    drained

6 black olives, pitted
    and halved

salt and pepper

1 lb/450 g dried linguine

1 oz/25 g/$^{1}/_{4}$ cup freshly
    grated Parmesan cheese

method

1 Heat the olive oil in a large skillet. Add the onions, garlic, and bacon, and cook over low heat, stirring occasionally, until the onions are softened. Stir in the mushrooms, anchovies, and olives, then season with salt, if necessary, and pepper. Let simmer for 5 minutes.

2 Meanwhile, bring a large heavy-bottom pan of lightly salted water to a boil. Add the pasta, return to a boil, and cook for 8–10 minutes, or until tender but still firm to the bite.

3 Drain the pasta and transfer to a warmed serving dish. Spoon the sauce on top, toss lightly, and sprinkle with the Parmesan cheese. Serve immediately.

saffron linguine

ingredients

SERVES 4

12 oz/350 g dried linguine

pinch of saffron threads

2 tbsp water

5 oz/140 g ham, cut into strips

6 fl oz/175 ml/³/₄ cup heavy
    cream

2 oz/55 g/¹/₂ cup freshly
    grated Parmesan cheese

salt and pepper

2 egg yolks

method

1 Bring a large heavy-bottom pan of lightly salted water to a boil. Add the pasta, return to a boil, and cook for 8–10 minutes, or until tender but still firm to the bite.

2 Meanwhile, place the saffron in a separate heavy-bottom pan and add the water. Bring to a boil, then remove from the heat and let stand for 5 minutes.

3 Stir the ham, cream, and grated Parmesan cheese into the saffron and return the pan to the heat. Season with salt and pepper and heat through gently, stirring constantly, until simmering. Remove the pan from the heat and beat in the egg yolks. Drain the pasta and transfer to a large, warmed serving dish. Add the saffron sauce, toss well, and serve.

rigatoni with ham, tomato & chile sauce

ingredients

SERVES 4

1 tbsp olive oil

2 tbsp butter

1 onion, chopped finely

5^1/$_2$ oz/150 g ham, diced

2 garlic cloves, chopped
  very finely

1 fresh red chile, seeded
  and chopped finely

1 lb 12 oz/800 g canned
  chopped tomatoes

salt and pepper

1 lb/450 g rigatoni or penne

2 tbsp chopped fresh flat-leaf
  parsley

6 tbsp freshly grated Parmesan
  cheese

method

1 Put the olive oil and 1 tablespoon of the butter in a large pan over medium-low heat. Add the onion and fry for 10 minutes until soft and golden. Add the ham and fry for 5 minutes until lightly browned. Stir in the garlic, chile, and tomatoes. Season with a little salt and pepper. Bring to a boil, then let simmer over medium-low heat for 30–40 minutes until thickened.

2 Cook the pasta in plenty of boiling salted water until tender but still firm to the bite. Drain and transfer to a warmed serving dish.

3 Pour the sauce over the pasta. Add the parsley, Parmesan cheese, and the remaining butter. Toss well to mix and serve immediately.

macaroni with sausage, pepperoncini & olives

ingredients

SERVES 4

1 tbsp olive oil

1 large onion, chopped finely

2 garlic cloves, minced

1 lb/450 g pork sausage, peeled and chopped coarsely

3 canned pepperoncini, or other hot red peppers, drained and sliced

14 oz/400 g canned chopped tomatoes

2 tsp dried oregano

4 fl oz/125 ml/$\frac{1}{2}$ cup chicken stock or red wine

salt and pepper

1 lb/450 g dried macaroni

12–15 black olives, pitted and cut into fourths

2$\frac{3}{4}$ oz/75 g/$\frac{1}{3}$ cup freshly grated cheese, such as Cheddar or Gruyère

method

1 Heat the oil in a large skillet over medium heat. Add the onion and fry for 5 minutes until soft. Add the garlic and fry for a few seconds until just beginning to color. Add the sausage and fry until evenly browned.

2 Stir in the pepperoncini, tomatoes, oregano, and stock. Season with salt and pepper. Bring to a boil, then let simmer over medium heat for 10 minutes, stirring occasionally.

3 Cook the macaroni in plenty of boiling salted water until tender but still firm to the bite. Drain and transfer to a warmed serving dish.

4 Add the olives and half the cheese to the sauce, then stir until the cheese has melted. Pour the sauce over the pasta. Toss well to mix. Sprinkle with the remaining cheese and serve at once.

pepperoni pasta

ingredients

SERVES 4

3 tbsp olive oil

1 onion, chopped

1 red bell pepper, seeded
   and diced

1 orange bell pepper, seeded
   and diced

1 lb 12 oz/800 g canned
   chopped tomatoes

1 tbsp sun-dried tomato paste

1 tsp paprika

8 oz/225 g pepperoni, sliced

2 tbsp chopped fresh flat-leaf
   parsley, plus extra to garnish

salt and pepper

1 lb/450 g dried garganelli

mixed salad greens, to serve

method

1 Heat 2 tablespoons of the olive oil in a large, heavy-bottom skillet. Add the onion and cook over low heat, stirring occasionally, for 5 minutes, or until softened. Add the red and orange bell peppers, tomatoes and their can juices, sun-dried tomato paste, and paprika to the pan and bring to a boil.

2 Add the pepperoni and parsley and season with salt and pepper. Stir well and bring to a boil, then reduce the heat and simmer for 10–15 minutes.

3 Meanwhile, bring a large, heavy-bottom pan of lightly salted water to a boil. Add the pasta, return to a boil, and cook for 8–10 minutes, or until tender but still firm to the bite. Drain well and transfer to a warmed serving dish. Add the remaining olive oil and toss. Add the sauce and toss again. Sprinkle with parsley and serve immediately with mixed salad greens.

chorizo & mushroom pasta

ingredients

SERVES 6

1 lb 8 oz/680 g dried vermicelli
4 fl oz/125 ml/$^1/_2$ cup olive oil
2 garlic cloves
4$^1/_2$ oz/125 g chorizo, sliced
8 oz/225 g exotic mushrooms
3 fresh red chiles, chopped
salt and pepper
2 tbsp fresh Parmesan cheese
  shavings, for sprinkling
10 anchovy fillets, to garnish

method

1 Bring a large, heavy-bottom pan of lightly salted water to a boil. Add the vermicelli, return to a boil and cook for 8–10 minutes, or until just tender, but still firm to the bite. Drain the pasta thoroughly, then place on a large, warmed serving plate and keep warm.

2 Meanwhile, heat the olive oil in a skillet. Add the garlic and cook for 1 minute. Add the chorizo and exotic mushrooms and cook for 4 minutes. Add the chopped chiles and cook for an additional 1 minute.

3 Pour the chorizo and exotic mushroom mixture over the vermicelli and season with salt and pepper. Sprinkle with fresh Parmesan cheese shavings, garnish with anchovy fillets, and serve at once.

linguine with lamb & yellow bell pepper sauce

ingredients

SERVES 4

4 tbsp olive oil

10 oz/280 g boneless lamb, cubed

1 garlic clove, finely chopped

1 bay leaf

8 fl oz/125ml/1 cup dry white wine

salt and pepper

2 large yellow bell peppers, seeded and diced

4 tomatoes, peeled and chopped

9 oz/250 g dried linguine

method

1 Heat half the olive oil in a large heavy-bottom skillet. Add the lamb and cook over medium heat, stirring frequently, until browned on all sides. Add the garlic and cook for an additional 1 minute. Add the bay leaf, pour in the wine, and season with salt and pepper. Bring to a boil and cook for 5 minutes, or until reduced.

2 Stir in the remaining oil, bell peppers, and tomatoes. Reduce the heat, cover, and let simmer, stirring occasionally, for 45 minutes.

3 Meanwhile, bring a large heavy-bottom pan of lightly salted water to a boil. Add the pasta, return to a boil, and cook for 8–10 minutes, or until tender but still firm to the bite. Drain and transfer to a warmed serving dish. Remove and discard the bay leaf from the lamb sauce and spoon the sauce onto the pasta. Toss well and serve immediately.

chicken with basil & pine nut pesto

ingredients

SERVES 4

2 tbsp vegetable oil

4 skinless, boneless
    chicken breasts

12 oz/350 g dried farfalle

salt and pepper

sprig of fresh basil, to garnish

pesto

3$\frac{1}{2}$ oz/100 g shredded
    fresh basil

4 fl oz/125 ml extra-virgin
    olive oil

3 tbsp pine nuts

3 garlic cloves, minced

2 oz/55 g freshly grated
    Parmesan cheese

2 tbsp freshly grated romano
    cheese

method

1 To make the pesto, place the basil, olive oil, pine nuts, garlic, and a generous pinch of salt in a food processor or blender and process until smooth. Scrape the mixture into a bowl and stir in the cheeses.

2 Heat the vegetable oil in a skillet over medium heat. Fry the chicken breasts, turning once, for 8–10 minutes until the juices are no longer pink. Cut into small cubes.

3 Cook the pasta in plenty of lightly salted boiling water until tender but still firm to the bite. Drain and transfer to a warmed serving dish. Add the chicken and pesto, then season with pepper. Toss well to mix.

4 Garnish with a basil sprig and serve warm.

tagliatelle with creamy chicken & shiitake sauce

ingredients

SERVES 4

1 oz/25 g/$^1/_3$ cup dried
    shiitake mushrooms
12 fl oz/350 ml/1$^1/_2$ cups
    hot water
1 tbsp olive oil
6 bacon strips, chopped
3 boneless, skinless chicken
    breasts, sliced into strips
4 oz/115 g/2 cups fresh
    shiitake mushrooms,
    sliced
1 small onion, chopped finely
1 tsp fresh oregano or
    marjoram, chopped finely
9 fl oz/275 ml/generous 1 cup
    chicken stock
10 fl oz/300 ml/1$^1/_4$ cups
    heavy cream
salt and pepper
1 lb/450 g dried tagliatelle
2 oz/55 g/$^1/_2$ cup freshly
    grated Parmesan cheese
chopped fresh flat-leaf
    parsley, to garnish

method

1 Put the dried mushrooms in a bowl with the hot water. Let soak for 30 minutes, or until softened. Remove, squeezing excess water back into the bowl. Strain the liquid in a fine-meshed strainer and reserve. Slice the soaked mushrooms, discarding the stems.

2 Heat the oil in a large skillet over a medium heat. Add the bacon and chicken, then stir-fry for about 3 minutes. Add the dried and fresh mushrooms, onion, and oregano. Stir-fry for 5–7 minutes, or until soft. Pour in the stock and the mushroom liquid. Bring to a boil, stirring. Simmer for about 10 minutes, continuing to stir, until reduced. Add the cream and simmer for 5 minutes, stirring, until beginning to thicken. Season with salt and pepper. Remove the skillet from the heat and set aside.

3 Cook the pasta until tender but still firm to the bite. Drain and transfer to a serving dish. Pour the sauce over the pasta. Add half the Parmesan cheese and mix. Sprinkle with parsley and serve with the remaining Parmesan cheese.

pappardelle with chicken & porcini

ingredients

SERVES 4

1¹/₂ oz/40 g dried porcini
  mushrooms

6 fl oz/175 ml/³/₄ cup hot
  water

1 lb 12 oz/800 g canned
  chopped tomatoes

1 fresh red chile, seeded
  and finely chopped

3 tbsp olive oil

12 oz/350 g skinless, boneless
  chicken, cut into thin strips

2 garlic cloves, finely chopped

12 oz/350 g dried pappardelle

salt and pepper

2 tbsp chopped fresh flat-leaf
  parsley, to garnish

method

1 Place the porcini in a small bowl, add the hot water, and let soak for 30 minutes. Meanwhile, place the tomatoes and their can juices in a heavy-bottom pan and break them up with a wooden spoon, then stir in the chile. Bring to a boil, then reduce the heat and let simmer, stirring occasionally, for 30 minutes, or until reduced.

2 Remove the mushrooms from their soaking liquid with a slotted spoon, reserving the liquid. Strain the liquid into the tomatoes, through a strainer lined with cheesecloth, and simmer for an additional 15 minutes. Meanwhile, heat 2 tablespoons of the olive oil in a heavy-bottom skillet. Add the chicken and cook, stirring frequently, until golden brown all over and tender. Stir in the mushrooms and garlic and cook for an additional 5 minutes.

3 Bring a large, heavy-bottom pan of lightly salted water to a boil. Add the pasta, return to a boil, and cook for 8–10 minutes, or until tender but still firm to the bite. Drain well, then transfer to a warmed serving dish. Drizzle the pasta with the remaining olive oil and toss lightly. Stir the chicken mixture into the tomato sauce, season with salt and pepper, and spoon onto the pasta. Toss lightly, sprinkle with parsley, and serve at once.

farfalle with chicken, broccoli & roasted red bell peppers

ingredients

SERVES 4

4 tbsp olive oil

5 tbsp butter

3 garlic cloves, chopped very
   finely

1 lb/450 g boneless, skinless
   chicken breasts, diced

1/4 tsp dried chile flakes

salt and pepper

1 lb/450 g small broccoli florets

10 1/2 oz/300 g/2 2/3 cups
   dried farfalle or fusilli

6 oz/175 g bottled roasted red
   bell peppers, drained
   and diced

9 fl oz/250 ml/generous 1 cup
   chicken stock

freshly grated Parmesan
   cheese, to serve (optional)

method

1 Bring a large pan of salted water to a boil. Meanwhile, place the olive oil, butter, and garlic in a large skillet over a medium-low heat. Cook the garlic until just beginning to color.

2 Add the diced chicken, then raise the heat to medium and stir-fry for 4–5 minutes, or until the chicken is no longer pink. Add the chile flakes and season with salt and pepper. Remove from the heat.

3 Plunge the broccoli into the boiling water and cook for 2 minutes, or until tender-crisp. Remove with a perforated spoon and set aside. Bring the water back to a boil. Add the pasta and cook until tender but still firm to the bite. Drain and add to the chicken mixture in the pan. Add the broccoli and roasted bell peppers, then pour in the stock. Let simmer briskly over medium-high heat, stirring frequently, until most of the liquid has been absorbed.

4 Serve sprinkled with the Parmesan cheese, if using.

spaghetti with parsley chicken

ingredients

SERVES 4

1 tbsp olive oil

thinly pared zest of 1 lemon, cut into julienne strips

1 tsp finely chopped fresh gingerroot

1 tsp sugar

salt

8 fl oz/250 ml/1 cup chicken stock

9 oz/250 g dried spaghetti

4 tbsp butter

8 oz/225 g skinless, boneless chicken breasts, diced

1 red onion, finely chopped

leaves from 2 bunches of flat-leaf parsley

method

1 Heat the olive oil in a heavy-bottom pan. Add most of the lemon zest, reserving a few strips to garnish, and cook over low heat, stirring frequently, for 5 minutes. Stir in the gingerroot and sugar, season with salt, and cook, stirring constantly, for an additional 2 minutes. Pour in the chicken stock, bring to a boil, then cook for 5 minutes, or until the liquid has reduced by half.

2 Meanwhile, bring a large heavy-bottom pan of lightly salted water to a boil. Add the pasta, return to a boil, and cook for 8–10 minutes, or until tender but still firm to the bite.

3 Meanwhile, melt half the butter in a skillet. Add the chicken and onion and cook, stirring frequently, for 5 minutes, or until the chicken is light brown all over. Stir in the lemon and ginger mixture and cook for 1 minute. Stir in the parsley leaves and cook, stirring constantly, for an additional 3 minutes.

4 Drain the pasta and transfer to a warmed serving dish, then add the remaining butter and toss well. Add the chicken sauce, toss again, and serve, garnished with the reserved lemon zest strips.

fettuccine with chicken & onion cream sauce

ingredients

SERVES 4

1 tbsp olive oil

2 tbsp butter

1 garlic clove, chopped
very finely

4 boneless, skinless chicken
breasts

salt and pepper

1 onion, chopped finely

1 chicken bouillon cube,
crumbled

4 fl oz/125 ml/^{1}/$_2$ cup water

10 fl oz/300 ml/1^1/$_4$ cups
heavy cream

6 fl oz/175 ml/^{3}/$_4$ cup milk

6 scallions, green part
included, sliced diagonally

1^1/$_4$ oz/35 g/scant ^{1}/$_3$ cup
freshly grated Parmesan
cheese

1 lb/450 g dried fettuccine

chopped fresh flat-leaf
parsley, to garnish

method

1 Heat the oil and butter with the garlic in a large skillet over a medium-low heat. Cook the garlic until just beginning to color. Add the chicken breasts and raise the heat to medium. Cook for 4–5 minutes on each side, or until the juices are no longer pink. Season with salt and pepper. Remove from the heat. Remove the chicken breasts, leaving the oil in the skillet. Slice the breasts diagonally into thin strips and set aside.

2 Reheat the oil in the skillet. Add the onion and cook gently for 5 minutes, or until soft. Add the crumbled bouillon cube and the water. Bring to a boil, then let simmer over a medium-low heat for 10 minutes. Stir in the cream, milk, scallions, and Parmesan cheese. Let simmer until heated through and slightly thickened.

3 Cook the fettuccine in boiling salted water until tender but still firm to the bite. Drain and transfer to a warmed serving dish. Layer the chicken slices over the pasta. Pour on the sauce, then garnish with parsley and serve.

creamy chicken ravioli

ingredients

SERVES 4

4 oz/115 g cooked skinless,
   boneless chicken breast,
   coarsely chopped
2 oz/55 g cooked spinach
2 oz/55 g prosciutto, coarsely
   chopped
1 shallot, coarsely chopped
6 tbsp freshly grated romano
   cheese
pinch of freshly grated nutmeg
2 eggs, lightly beaten
salt and pepper
1 quantity basic pasta dough
   (see below)
all-purpose flour,
   for dusting
10 fl oz/300 ml/1¼ cups
   heavy cream
2 garlic cloves,
   finely chopped
4 oz/115 g cremini
   mushrooms, thinly sliced
2 tbsp shredded fresh basil
fresh basil sprigs, to garnish

pasta dough

7 oz/200 g/1 cup all-purpose
   flour, plus extra for dusting
pinch of salt
2 eggs, lightly beaten
1 tbsp olive oil

method

1 To make the pasta dough, sift the flour into a food processor. Add the salt, eggs, and olive oil and process until the dough begins to come together. Knead on a lightly floured counter until smooth. Cover and let rest for 30 minutes.

2 Process the chicken, spinach, prosciutto, and shallot in a food processor until chopped and blended. Transfer to a bowl, stir in 2 tablespoons of the romano cheese, the nutmeg, and half the egg, and season.

3 Halve the pasta dough. Thinly roll out one half on a lightly floured counter. Cover with a dish towel and roll out the second half. Place small mounds of the filling in rows 1½ inches/ 4 cm apart on one sheet of dough and brush in between with beaten egg. Cover with the other half of dough. Press down between the mounds of filling, pushing out any air. Cut into squares and let rest on a floured dish towel for 1 hour.

4 Bring a pan of lightly salted water to a boil. Add the ravioli, in batches, return to a boil, and cook for 5 minutes. Remove and drain on paper towels, then transfer to a warmed dish.

5 Meanwhile, bring the cream to a boil with the garlic in a skillet. Let simmer for 1 minute, then add the mushrooms and 2 tablespoons of the remaining cheese. Season, then let simmer for 3 minutes. Stir in the basil, then pour the sauce over the ravioli. Sprinkle with the remaining cheese, garnish with basil sprigs, and serve.

chicken tortellini

ingredients

SERVES 4

4 oz/115 g skinless, boneless
   chicken breast

2 oz/55 g prosciutto

1¹/₂ oz/40 g cooked spinach,
   well drained

1 tbsp finely
   chopped onion

2 tbsp freshly grated
   Parmesan cheese

pinch of ground allspice

1 egg, beaten

salt and pepper

double quantity pasta dough
   (see page 86)

2 tbsp chopped fresh
   flat-leaf parsley, to garnish

sauce

10 fl oz/300 ml/1¹/₄ cups
   light cream

2 garlic cloves, crushed

4 oz/115 g white mushrooms,
   thinly sliced

salt and pepper

4 tbsp freshly grated
   Parmesan cheese

method

1 Bring a pan of lightly salted water to a boil. Add the chicken and poach for 10 minutes. Let cool slightly, then place in a food processor with the prosciutto, spinach, and onion and process until finely chopped. Stir in the Parmesan cheese, allspice, and egg and season with salt and pepper.

2 Thinly roll out the pasta dough and cut into 1¹/₂–2-inch/4–5-cm circles. Place ¹/₂ teaspoon of the chicken and ham filling in the center of each circle. Fold the pieces in half and press the edges to seal, then wrap each piece around your index finger, cross over the ends, and curl the rest of the dough backward to make a navel shape. Re-roll the trimmings and repeat until all the dough is used up.

3 Bring a pan of salted water to a boil. Add the tortellini, in batches, return to a boil, and cook for 5 minutes. Drain the tortellini well and transfer to a serving dish.

4 To make the sauce, bring the cream and garlic to a boil in a small pan, then simmer for 3 minutes. Add the mushrooms and half the cheese, season with salt and pepper, and simmer for 2–3 minutes. Pour the sauce over the tortellini. Sprinkle over the remaining Parmesan cheese, garnish with the parsley, and serve.

seafood

Pasta combined with seafood gives a light, elegant, delicate result that is ideal for midweek suppers and for lunch parties. Even when the recipe calls for a fairly robust pasta, such as Mafalde with Fresh Salmon, Fusilli with Monkfish & Broccoli, or Springtime Pasta, you will finish your meal feeling comfortably satisfied and your digestive system will not be overwhelmed.

A great store-cupboard standby is Pasta with Tuna, Garlic, Lemon, Capers & Olives—if you keep a pot of fresh parsley growing on your windowsill, you can be ready to make this quick dish any time. When a stylish recipe is the order of the day, dishes such as Fettuccine with Sole & Monkfish, Linguine with Smoked Salmon & Arugula, Crab Ravioli, and Fettuccine with Scallops in Porcini & Cream Sauce are perfect—they almost look too good to eat. If you are passionate about shellfish, try Mixed Shellfish with Angel-hair Pasta, Spaghetti with Clams, Tagliatelle & Mussels with White Wine, Garlic & Parsley, or Seafood Pasta Pockets—you can serve these in the parchment paper packages they are cooked in.

Fusion food is now very popular and an excellent example of how well this can work is Fusilli with Hot Cajun Seafood Sauce—it's completely cross-cultural and tastes absolutely divine!

fettuccine with sole & monkfish

ingredients

SERVES 4

3 oz/85 g/generous ¹/₂ cup
   all-purpose flour

salt and pepper

1 lb/450 g lemon sole fillets,
   skinned and cut into chunks

1 lb/450 g monkfish fillets,
   skinned and cut into chunks

3 oz/85 g unsalted butter

4 shallots, finely chopped

2 garlic cloves, crushed

1 carrot, diced

1 leek, finely chopped

10 fl oz/300 ml/1¹/₄ cups
   fish stock

10 fl oz/300 ml/1¹/₄ cups
   dry white wine

2 tsp anchovy essence

1 tbsp balsamic vinegar

1 lb/450 g dried fettuccine

chopped fresh flat-leaf
   parsley, to garnish

method

1 Season the flour with salt and pepper and spread out 2 tablespoons on a plate. Coat all the fish pieces with it, shaking off the excess. Melt the butter in a heavy-bottom pan or flameproof casserole. Add the fish, shallots, garlic, carrot, and leek, then cook over low heat, stirring frequently, for 10 minutes. Sprinkle in the remaining seasoned flour and cook, stirring constantly, for 1 minute.

2 Mix the fish stock, wine, anchovy essence, and balsamic vinegar together in a pitcher and gradually stir into the fish mixture. Bring to a boil, stirring constantly, then reduce the heat and let simmer gently for 35 minutes.

3 Meanwhile, bring a large heavy-bottom pan of lightly salted water to a boil. Add the pasta, return to a boil, and cook for 8–10 minutes, or until tender but still firm to the bite. Drain and transfer to a warmed serving dish. Spoon the fish mixture onto the pasta, garnish with chopped parsley, and serve immediately.

linguine with smoked salmon & arugula

ingredients

SERVES 4

12 oz/350 g dried linguine

2 tbsp olive oil

1 garlic clove, finely chopped

4 oz/115 g smoked salmon,
    cut into thin strips

2 oz/55 g arugula

salt and pepper

4 lemon halves, to garnish

method

1 Bring a large, heavy-bottom pan of lightly salted water to a boil. Add the pasta, return to a boil, and cook for 8–10 minutes, or until tender but still firm to the bite.

2 Just before the end of the cooking time, heat the olive oil in a heavy-bottom skillet. Add the garlic and cook over low heat, stirring constantly, for 1 minute. Do not allow the garlic to brown or it will taste bitter. Add the salmon and arugula. Season with salt and pepper and cook, stirring constantly, for 1 minute. Remove the skillet from the heat.

3 Drain the pasta and transfer to a warmed dish. Add the smoked salmon and arugula mixture, toss lightly and serve, garnished with lemon halves.

conchiglie with smoked salmon, sour cream & mustard sauce

ingredients

SERVES 4

1 lb/450 g conchiglie or
   tagliatelle

10 fl oz/300 ml/1^1/$_4$ cups
   sour cream

2 tsp Dijon mustard

4 large scallions, sliced finely

8 oz/225 g smoked salmon,
   cut into bite-sized pieces

finely grated rind of ^{1}/$_2$ lemon

pepper

2 tbsp chopped fresh chives
   plus whole chives, to
   garnish

method

1 Cook the pasta in plenty of boiling salted water until tender but still firm to the bite. Drain and return to the pan. Add the sour cream, mustard, scallions, smoked salmon, and lemon rind to the pasta. Stir over low heat until heated through. Season with pepper.

2 Transfer to a serving dish. Sprinkle with the chopped chives. Serve warm or at room temperature, garnished with whole chives.

mafalde with fresh salmon

ingredients

SERVES 4

12 oz/350 g salmon fillet

fresh dill sprigs, plus extra
     to garnish

8 fl oz/125ml/1 cup
     dry white wine

salt and pepper

6 tomatoes, peeled
     and chopped

5 fl oz/150 ml/^{2}/$_3$ cup heavy
     cream

12 oz/350 g dried mafalde,
     tagliatelle, or fettuccine

4 oz/115 g cooked, shelled
     shrimp

method

1 Place the salmon in a large heavy-bottom skillet. Add a few dill sprigs, pour in the wine, and season with salt and pepper. Bring to a boil, then reduce the heat, cover, and poach gently for 5 minutes, or until the flesh flakes easily. Remove with a spatula, reserving the cooking liquid, and let cool slightly. Remove and discard the skin and any remaining small bones, then flake the flesh into large chunks.

2 Add the tomatoes and cream to the reserved liquid. Bring to a boil, then reduce the heat and let simmer for 15 minutes, or until the sauce has thickened.

3 Meanwhile, bring a large heavy-bottom pan of lightly salted water to a boil. Add the pasta, return to a boil, and cook for 8–10 minutes, or until tender but still firm to the bite. Drain and transfer to a warmed serving dish.

4 Add the salmon and shrimp to the tomato sauce and stir gently until coated. Spoon the sauce onto the pasta, toss lightly, then serve, garnished with dill sprigs.

italian fish stew with ziti

ingredients

SERVES 4

pinch of saffron threads
32 fl oz/1 liter/4 cups
    fish stock
4 tbsp butter
1 lb/450 g red snapper fillets,
    thinly sliced
12 prepared scallops
12 raw jumbo shrimp, shelled
    and deveined
8 oz/225 g raw shrimp,
    shelled and deveined
salt and pepper
finely grated rind and juice
    of 1 lemon
5 fl oz/150 ml/^{2}/$_3$ cup white
    wine vinegar
5 fl oz/150 ml/^{2}/$_3$ cup white
    wine
5 fl oz/150 ml/^{2}/$_3$ cup heavy
    cream
3 tbsp chopped fresh flat-leaf
    parsley
1 lb/450 g dried ziti

method

1 Place the saffron in a small bowl, add 3 tablespoons of the fish stock, and let soak. Melt the butter in a large heavy-bottom pan or flameproof casserole. Add the red snapper, scallops, and both types of shrimp and cook over medium heat, stirring frequently, for 3–5 minutes, or until the shrimp have changed color. Season with pepper and add the grated rind and lemon juice. Transfer the fish and shellfish to a plate and keep warm.

2 Pour the remaining stock into the pan and add the saffron and its soaking liquid. Bring to a boil and cook until reduced by about one third. Add the vinegar and continue to boil for 4 minutes. Stir in the white wine and cook for 5 minutes, or until reduced and thickened. Add the cream and parsley, then season with salt and pepper and let simmer gently for 2 minutes.

3 Meanwhile, bring a large heavy-bottom pan of lightly salted water to a boil. Add the pasta, return to a boil, and cook for 8–10 minutes, or until tender but still firm to the bite. Drain well and transfer to a large, warmed serving platter. Arrange the fish and shellfish on top and pour over the sauce. Serve immediately.

fusilli with monkfish & broccoli

ingredients

SERVES 4

4 oz/115 g head of broccoli, divided into florets

3 tbsp olive oil

12 oz/350 g monkfish fillet, skinned and cut into bite-size pieces

2 garlic cloves, crushed

salt and pepper

4 fl oz/125 ml/$\frac{1}{2}$ cup dry white wine

8 fl oz/225 ml/1 cup heavy cream

14 oz/400 g dried fusilli bucati

3 oz/85 g Gorgonzola cheese, diced

method

1 Divide the broccoli florets into tiny sprigs. Bring a pan of lightly salted water to a boil, add the broccoli, and cook for 2 minutes. Drain and refresh under cold running water.

2 Heat the olive oil in a large heavy-bottom skillet. Add the monkfish and garlic and season with salt and pepper. Cook, stirring frequently, for 5 minutes, or until the fish is opaque. Pour in the white wine and cream and cook, stirring occasionally, for 5 minutes, or until the fish is cooked through and the sauce has thickened. Stir in the broccoli sprigs.

3 Meanwhile, bring a large heavy-bottom pan of lightly salted water to a boil. Add the pasta, return to a boil, and cook for 8–10 minutes, or until tender but still firm to the bite. Drain the pasta and tip it into the pan with the fish, add the cheese, and toss lightly. Serve immediately.

penne with squid & tomatoes

ingredients

SERVES 4

8 oz/225 g dried penne

12 oz/350 g prepared squid

6 tbsp olive oil

2 onions, sliced

8 fl oz/250 ml/1 cup fish or
  chicken stock

5 fl oz/150 ml/^{2}/$_3$ cup full-
  bodied red wine

14 oz/400 g canned chopped
  tomatoes

2 tbsp tomato paste

1 tbsp chopped fresh marjoram

1 bay leaf

salt and pepper

2 tbsp chopped fresh parsley

method

1 Bring a large heavy-bottom pan of lightly salted water to a boil. Add the pasta, return to a boil, and cook for 3 minutes, then drain and set aside until required. With a sharp knife, cut the squid into strips.

2 Heat the olive oil in a large flameproof dish or casserole. Add the onions and cook over low heat, stirring occasionally, for 5 minutes, or until softened. Add the squid and fish stock, bring to a boil, and let simmer for 3 minutes. Stir in the wine, chopped tomatoes and their can juices, tomato paste, marjoram, and bay leaf. Season with salt and pepper. Bring to a boil and cook for 5 minutes, or until slightly reduced.

3 Add the pasta, return to a boil, and let simmer for 5–7 minutes, or until tender but still firm to the bite. Remove and discard the bay leaf, stir in the parsley, and serve at once.

pasta with tuna, garlic, lemon, capers & olives

ingredients

SERVES 4

12 oz/350 g dried conchiglie
  or gnocchi

4 tbsp olive oil

4 tbsp butter

3 large garlic cloves,
  sliced thinly

7 oz/200 g canned tuna,
  drained and broken
  into chunks

2 tbsp lemon juice

1 tbsp capers, drained

10–12 black olives, pitted
  and sliced

2 tbsp chopped fresh flat-leaf
  parsley, to serve

method

1 Cook the pasta or gnocchi in plenty of boiling salted water until tender but still firm to the bite. Drain and return to the pan.

2 Heat the olive oil and half the butter in a skillet over medium-low heat. Add the garlic and cook for a few seconds until just beginning to color. Reduce the heat to low. Add the tuna, lemon juice, capers, and olives. Stir gently until all the ingredients are heated through.

3 Transfer the pasta or gnocchi to a warmed serving dish. Pour the tuna mixture over the pasta. Add the parsley and remaining butter. Toss well to mix, then serve immediately.

spaghetti with tuna & parsley

ingredients

SERVES 4

1 lb 2 oz/500 g dried
    spaghetti
1 oz/25 g butter
fresh flat-leaf parsley sprigs,
    to garnish
black olives, to serve
    (optional)

sauce

7 oz/200 g canned tuna,
    drained
2 oz/55 g canned anchovies,
    drained
9 fl oz/250 ml/1 cup olive oil
2 oz/55 g coarsely chopped
    fresh flat-leaf parsley
5 fl oz/150 ml/^{2}/$_3$ cup sour
    cream or yogurt
salt and pepper

method

1 Bring a large, heavy-bottom pan of lightly salted water to a boil. Add the spaghetti, return to a boil, and cook for 8–10 minutes, or until tender but still firm to the bite. Drain the spaghetti in a colander and return to the pan. Add the butter, toss thoroughly to coat, and keep warm until required.

2 Flake the tuna into smaller pieces using 2 forks. Place the tuna in a blender or food processor with the anchovies, olive oil, and parsley and process until the sauce is smooth. Pour in the sour cream or yogurt and process for a few seconds to blend. Taste the sauce and season with salt and pepper, if necessary.

3 Warm 4 plates. Shake the pan of spaghetti over medium heat for a few minutes, or until it is thoroughly warmed through.

4 Pour the sauce over the spaghetti and toss quickly, using 2 forks. Garnish with the flat-leaf parsley and serve immediately with a small dish of black olives, if liked.

linguine alla puttanesca

ingredients

SERVES 4

1 lb/450 g plum tomatoes

3 tbsp olive oil

2 garlic cloves, finely chopped

10 anchovy fillets, drained
    and chopped

5 oz/140 g/¾ cup black
    olives, pitted and chopped

1 tbsp capers, rinsed

pinch of cayenne pepper

14 oz/400 g dried linguine

salt

2 tbsp chopped fresh flat-leaf
    parsley, to garnish

crusty bread, to serve

method

1 Peel the tomatoes by cutting a cross in the bottom of each and placing in a heatproof bowl. Cover with boiling water and let stand for 35–45 seconds. Drain and plunge into cold water, then the skins will slide off easily. Seed and chop the tomatoes.

2 Heat the olive oil in a heavy-bottom pan. Add the garlic and cook over low heat, stirring frequently, for 2 minutes. Add the anchovies and mash them to a pulp with a fork. Add the olives, capers, and tomatoes and season with cayenne pepper. Cover and let simmer for 25 minutes.

3 Meanwhile, bring a pan of lightly salted water to a boil. Add the pasta, return to a boil, and cook for 8–10 minutes, or until tender but still firm to the bite. Drain and transfer to a warmed serving dish.

4 Spoon the anchovy sauce into the dish and toss the pasta, using 2 large forks. Garnish with the parsley and serve immediately with crusty bread.

spinach & anchovy pasta

ingredients

SERVES 4

2 lb/900 g fresh, young
spinach leaves
14 oz/400 g dried fettuccine
5 tbsp olive oil
3 tbsp pine nuts
3 garlic cloves, crushed
8 canned anchovy fillets,
drained and chopped

method

1 Trim off any tough spinach stalks. Rinse the spinach leaves under cold running water and place them in a large pan with only the water that is clinging to them after washing. Cover and cook over high heat, shaking the pan from time to time, until the spinach has wilted, but retains its color. Drain well, set aside, and keep warm.

2 Bring a large heavy-bottom pan of lightly salted water to a boil. Add the fettuccine, return to a boil and cook for 8–10 minutes, or until it is just tender but still firm to the bite.

3 Heat 4 tablespoons of the olive oil in a separate pan. Add the pine nuts and cook until golden. Remove the pine nuts from the pan and set aside.

4 Add the garlic to the pan and cook until golden. Add the anchovies and stir in the spinach. Cook, stirring, for 2–3 minutes, until heated through. Return the pine nuts to the pan.

5 Drain the fettuccine, toss in the remaining olive oil and transfer to a warmed serving dish. Spoon the anchovy and spinach sauce over the fettuccine, toss lightly, and serve at once.

crab ravioli

ingredients

SERVES 4

6 scallions

12 oz/350 g cooked crabmeat

2 tsp finely chopped
  fresh gingerroot

$1/8$–$1/4$ tsp chili or Tabasco
  sauce

1 lb 9 oz/700 g tomatoes,
  peeled, seeded, and
  coarsely chopped

1 garlic clove, finely chopped

1 tbsp white wine vinegar

1 quantity basic pasta dough
  (see below)

all-purpose flour, for dusting

1 egg, lightly beaten

2 tbsp heavy cream

salt

shredded scallion, to garnish

pasta dough

7 oz/200 g/1 cup all-purpose
  flour, plus extra for dusting

pinch of salt

2 eggs, lightly beaten

1 tbsp olive oil

method

1 To make the pasta dough, sift the flour into a food processor. Add the salt, eggs, and olive oil and process until the dough begins to come together. Knead on a lightly floured counter until smooth. Cover and let rest for 30 minutes.

2 Thinly slice the scallions, keeping the white and green parts separate. Mix the green scallions, crabmeat, gingerroot, and chili sauce in a bowl. Cover and let chill.

3 Process the tomatoes in a food processor to a purée. Place the garlic, white scallions, and vinegar in a pan and add the puréed tomatoes. Bring to a boil, stirring, then let simmer gently for 10 minutes. Remove from the heat.

4 Thinly roll out half of the pasta dough on a lightly floured counter. Cover with a dish towel and roll out the other half. Place small mounds of the filling in rows $1^{1}/2$ inches/4 cm apart on one sheet of dough and brush in between with beaten egg. Cover with the other half of dough. Press down between the mounds, cut into squares, and let rest on a dish towel for 1 hour.

5 Bring a large pan of lightly salted water to a boil. Add the ravioli, in batches, return to a boil, and cook for 5 minutes. Remove with a slotted spoon and drain on paper towels. Meanwhile, gently heat the tomato sauce and whisk in the cream. Serve the ravioli with the sauce poured over and garnished with shredded scallion.

spaghetti with clams

ingredients

SERVES 4

2 lb 4 oz/1 kg live clams,
    scrubbed under cold
    running water*

6 fl oz/175 ml/³/₄ cup water

6 fl oz/175 ml/³/₄ cup dry
    white wine

12 oz/350 g dried spaghetti

5 tbsp olive oil

2 garlic cloves, finely chopped

4 tbsp chopped fresh
    flat-leaf parsley

salt and pepper

* discard any clams with
broken or damaged shells
and any that do not shut
when sharply tapped

method

1 Place the clams in a large, heavy-bottom pan, add the water and wine, cover, and cook over high heat, shaking the pan occasionally, for 5 minutes, or until the shells have opened.

2 Remove the clams with a slotted spoon and let cool slightly. Strain the cooking liquid, through a strainer lined with cheesecloth, into a small pan. Bring to a boil and cook until reduced by about half, then remove from the heat. Meanwhile, discard any clams that have not opened, remove the remainder from their shells, and reserve until required.

3 Bring a large pan of lightly salted water to a boil. Add the pasta, return to a boil, and cook for 8–10 minutes, or until tender but still firm to the bite.

4 Meanwhile, heat the olive oil in a large, heavy-bottom skillet. Add the garlic and cook, stirring frequently, for 2 minutes. Add the parsley and the reduced clam cooking liquid and let simmer gently.

5 Drain the pasta and add it to the skillet with the clams. Season with salt and pepper and cook, stirring constantly, for 4 minutes, or until the pasta is coated and the clams have heated through. Transfer to a warmed serving dish and serve immediately.

tagliatelle & mussels with white wine, garlic & parsley

ingredients

SERVES 4

4 lb 8 oz/2 kilos mussels, scrubbed

1 large onion, chopped

3 garlic cloves, minced

18 fl oz/550 ml/2¼ cups dry white wine

1 bay leaf

2 sprigs of fresh thyme

5 tbsp chopped fresh flat-leaf parsley

1 tbsp chopped fresh rosemary

4 tbsp butter

salt and pepper

1 lb/450 g dried tagliatelle or other broad-ribboned pasta

method

1 Clean the mussels by scrubbing the shells and pulling out any beards that are attached. Rinse well, discarding any with broken shells or that remain open when tapped.

2 Put the onion, garlic, white wine, herbs, and 2 tablespoons of the butter in a pan. Bring to a boil, then reduce the heat. Add the mussels, then season with salt and pepper. Cover and cook over medium heat for 3–4 minutes, shaking the pan, until the mussels open. Remove from the heat. Lift out the mussels with a perforated spoon, reserving the liquid. Discard any that remain closed. Remove most of the others from their shells, reserving a few in their shells to garnish.

3 Cook the pasta until tender but still firm to the bite, then drain it and divide it among 4 individual serving bowls. Spoon the mussels over the pasta. Strain the mussel liquid and return to the pan. Add the remaining butter and heat until melted. Pour over the pasta, garnish with the mussels in their shells, and serve immediately.

mixed shellfish with angel-hair pasta

ingredients

SERVES 4

3 oz/85 g prepared squid

1 tsp cornstarch

1 tbsp water

1 egg white

4 prepared scallops, sliced

3 oz/85 g raw shrimp, shelled
    and deveined

salt

12 oz/350 g angel-hair pasta

3 tbsp peanut oil

2 oz/55 g snow peas

1 tbsp dark soy sauce

1 tbsp dry sherry

1/2 tsp light brown sugar

2 scallions, shredded

method

1 Open out the squid and, with a sharp knife, score the inside with criss-cross lines. Cut into small pieces, about 3/4-inch/2-cm square. Place in a bowl and cover with boiling water. When the squares have curled up, drain and rinse in cold water. Mix the cornstarch and water together in a small bowl until a smooth paste forms and stir in about half the egg white. Add the scallops and shrimp and toss until well coated.

2 Bring a large heavy-bottom pan of lightly salted water to a boil. Add the pasta, return to a boil, and cook for 5 minutes, or until tender but still firm to the bite.

3 Meanwhile, heat the oil in a preheated wok or heavy-bottom skillet. Add the snow peas, squid, scallops, and shrimp, and stir-fry for 2 minutes. Stir in the soy sauce, sherry, sugar, and scallions, and cook, stirring, for 1 minute. Drain the pasta and divide it among 4 warmed plates. Top with the shellfish mixture and serve at once.

spaghetti & shellfish

ingredients

SERVES 4

8 oz/225 g dried short-cut
   spaghetti, or long
   spaghetti broken into
   6-inch/15-cm lengths
1 tbsp olive oil
10 fl oz/300 ml/1^{1}/$_{4}$ cups
   chicken stock
1 tsp lemon juice
1 small cauliflower,
   cut into florets
2 carrots, sliced thinly
4^{1}/$_{2}$ oz/125 g snow peas
2 oz/55 g butter
1 onion, sliced
8 oz/225 g zucchini,
   thinly sliced
1 garlic clove, chopped
12 oz/350 g frozen shelled
   shrimp, thawed
salt and pepper
2 tbsp chopped fresh parsley
1 oz/25 g/^{1}/$_{4}$ cup freshly
   grated Parmesan cheese
^{1}/$_{2}$ tsp paprika, to sprinkle
4 unshelled shrimp, to
   garnish (optional)
crusty bread, to serve

method

1 Bring a large, heavy-bottom pan of lightly salted water to a boil. Add the spaghetti, return to a boil and cook for 8–10 minutes, or until tender but still firm to the bite. Drain, then return to the pan and stir in the olive oil. Cover and keep warm.

2 Bring the chicken stock and lemon juice to a boil. Add the cauliflower and carrots and cook for 3–4 minutes, until they are tender. Remove with a slotted spoon and set aside. Add the snow peas and cook for 1–2 minutes, until they start to soften. Remove and add to the other vegetables. Reserve the stock for future use.

3 Melt half of the butter in a skillet over medium heat and cook the onion and zucchini for 3 minutes. Add the garlic and shrimp and cook for an additional 2–3 minutes, until thoroughly heated through.

4 Stir in the reserved vegetables and heat through. Season with salt and pepper, then stir in the remaining butter. Transfer the spaghetti to a warmed serving dish. Pour on the sauce and parsley. Toss well using 2 forks, until thoroughly coated. Sprinkle on the grated cheese and paprika, and garnish with unshelled shrimp, if using. Serve immediately, with crusty bread.

spaghetti with shrimp

ingredients

SERVES 4

1 lb/450 g dried spaghetti

4 fl oz/125 ml/^{1}/$_2$ cup olive oil

6 garlic cloves, sliced thinly

1 lb/450 g raw medium
   shrimp, shelled and
   deveined

2 tbsp flat-leaf parsley,
   chopped finely, plus
   2 tbsp extra, to garnish

4 fl oz/125 ml/^{1}/$_2$ cup dry
   white wine

4 tbsp freshly squeezed
   lemon juice

salt and pepper

method

1 Bring a large pan of salted water to a boil over high heat. Add the spaghetti, return the water to a boil, and boil for 10 minutes, or until tender.

2 Meanwhile, heat the oil in another large pan over medium heat. Add the garlic and cook until just golden brown. Add the shrimp and 2 tablespoons of chopped parsley and stir. Add the wine and let simmer for 2 minutes. Stir in the lemon juice and let simmer until the shrimp turn pink and curl.

3 Drain the spaghetti, then tip it into the pan with the shrimp and toss. Season with salt and pepper.

4 Transfer to a large serving platter and sprinkle with the extra parsley. Serve at once.

seafood pasta pockets

ingredients

SERVES 4

2 tbsp virgin olive oil

2 fresh red chiles, seeded
and finely chopped

4 garlic cloves, finely chopped

1 lb 12 oz/800 g canned
tomatoes

8 fl oz/225ml/1 cup
dry white wine

salt and pepper

12 oz/350 g dried spaghetti

2 tbsp butter

4 oz/115 g prepared raw squid,
sliced

6 oz/175 g raw jumbo shrimp

1 lb/450 g live mussels,
scrubbed and debearded*

1 crab, about 3 lb 5 oz/1.5 kg,
freshly cooked, all meat
removed

3 tbsp coarsely chopped
fresh flat-leaf parsley

1 tbsp shredded fresh basil
leaves

* discard any damaged
mussels or any that do not
shut immediately when
tapped; once cooked,
discard any mussels that
remain closed

method

1 Heat 1 tablespoon of the olive oil in a large pan. Add half the chiles and half the garlic, and cook over medium heat, stirring occasionally, for 2–3 minutes. Add the tomatoes with their can juices and the wine. Reduce the heat and let simmer for about 1 hour. Strain the sauce, season, and set aside.

2 Bring a pan of lightly salted water to a boil. Add the pasta, return to a boil, and cook for 8–10 minutes, until tender but still firm to the bite.

3 Heat the remaining olive oil with the butter in a large, heavy-bottom pan. Add the remaining chile and garlic and cook over low heat, stirring occasionally, for 5 minutes, or until softened. Add the squid, shrimp, and mussels, cover the pan, and cook over high heat for 4–5 minutes, or until the mussels have opened. Remove the pan from the heat and stir in the crab meat.

4 Drain the pasta and add it to the seafood with the chile and tomato sauce, parsley, and basil, tossing well to coat.

5 Cut out 4 large squares of parchment paper. Divide the pasta and seafood among them, placing it on one half. Fold over the other half and turn in the edges securely to seal. Transfer to a large cookie sheet and bake in a preheated oven, 350°F/180°C, for 10 minutes, or until the pockets have puffed up. Serve at once.

spaghetti with shrimp & garlic sauce

ingredients

SERVES 4

3 tbsp olive oil

3 tbsp butter

4 garlic cloves, minced

2 tbsp finely diced red
bell pepper

2 tbsp tomato paste

4 fl oz/125 ml/$\frac{1}{2}$ cup
dry white wine

1 lb/450 g spaghetti or
tagliatelle

12 oz/350 g raw shelled shrimp

4 fl oz/125 ml/$\frac{1}{2}$ cup heavy
cream

salt and pepper

3 tbsp chopped fresh flat-leaf
parsley, to garnish

method

1 Heat the oil and butter in a pan over medium-low heat. Add the garlic and red bell pepper. Fry for a few seconds until the garlic is just beginning to color. Stir in the tomato paste and wine. Cook for 10 minutes, stirring.

2 Cook the spaghetti in plenty of boiling salted water until tender but still firm to the bite. Drain and return to the pan.

3 Add the shrimp to the sauce and raise the heat to medium-high. Cook for 2 minutes, stirring, until the shrimp turn pink. Reduce the heat and stir in the cream. Cook for 1 minute, stirring constantly, until thickened. Season with salt and pepper.

4 Transfer the spaghetti to a warmed serving dish and pour over the sauce. Sprinkle with the parsley. Toss well to mix and serve at once.

springtime pasta

ingredients

SERVES 4

2 tbsp lemon juice

4 baby globe artichokes

7 tbsp olive oil

2 shallots, finely chopped

2 garlic cloves, finely chopped

2 tbsp chopped fresh flat-leaf parsley

2 tbsp chopped fresh mint

12 oz/350 g dried rigatoni or other tubular pasta

2 tbsp unsalted butter

12 large raw shrimp, shelled and deveined

salt and pepper

method

1 Fill a large bowl with cold water and add the lemon juice. Prepare the artichokes one at a time. Cut off the stems and trim away any tough outer leaves. Cut across the tops of the leaves. Slice in half lengthwise and remove the central fibrous chokes, then cut lengthwise into slices 1/4 inch/5 mm thick. Immediately place the slices in the bowl of acidulated water to prevent discoloration.

2 Heat 5 tablespoons of the olive oil in a heavy-bottom skillet. Drain the artichoke slices and pat dry with paper towels. Add them to the skillet with the shallots, garlic, parsley, and mint and cook over low heat, stirring frequently, for 10–12 minutes, or until tender.

3 Meanwhile, bring a large pan of lightly salted water to a boil. Add the pasta, return to a boil, and cook for 8–10 minutes, or until tender but still firm to the bite.

4 Melt the butter in a skillet, cut the shrimp in half, and add them to the skillet. Cook, stirring occasionally, for 2–3 minutes, or until the shrimp have changed color. Season with salt and pepper.

5 Drain the pasta and tip it into a bowl. Add the remaining olive oil and toss well. Add the artichoke mixture and the shrimp and toss again. Serve immediately.

tagliatelle with shrimp, tomatoes, garlic & chile

ingredients

SERVES 4

4 tbsp olive oil

5 garlic cloves, chopped
very finely

14 oz/400 g canned chopped
tomatoes

1 fresh red chile, seeded
and chopped very finely

salt and pepper

1 lb/450 g dried tagliatelle
or spaghetti

12 oz/350 g raw shelled shrimp

2 tbsp chopped fresh flat-leaf
parsley, plus extra to
garnish

method

1 Heat 2 tablespoons of the oil and the garlic in a pan over a medium-low heat. Cook the garlic until just beginning to color. Add the tomatoes and chile. Bring to a boil, then let simmer over medium-low heat for 30 minutes until the oil separates from the tomatoes. Season with salt and pepper.

2 Cook the pasta in plenty of boiling salted water until tender but still firm to the bite. Drain and return to the pan.

3 Heat the remaining oil in a skillet over high heat. Add the shrimp and stir-fry for 2 minutes until pink. Add the shrimp to the tomato mixture. Stir in the parsley, then let simmer over low heat until bubbling.

4 Transfer the pasta to a warmed serving dish. Pour the sauce over the pasta. Toss well to mix. Garnish with chopped parsley and serve immediately.

fusilli with hot cajun seafood sauce

ingredients

SERVES 4

18 fl oz/500 ml/2^{1}/$_{4}$ cups heavy
   cream
8 scallions, sliced thinly
2 oz/55 g chopped fresh
   flat-leaf parsley
1 tbsp chopped fresh thyme
^{1}/$_{2}$ tbsp pepper
^{1}/$_{2}$–1 tsp dried chile flakes
1 tsp salt
1 lb/450 g dried fusilli or
   tagliatelle
1^{1}/$_{2}$ oz/40 g/^{1}/$_{3}$ cup freshly
   grated Gruyère cheese
1 oz/25 g/^{1}/$_{4}$ cup freshly
   grated Parmesan cheese
2 tbsp olive oil
8 oz/225 g raw shelled
   shrimp
8 oz/225 g scallops, sliced
1 tbsp shredded fresh basil,
   to serve

method

1 Heat the cream in a large pan over medium heat, stirring constantly. When almost boiling, reduce the heat and add the scallions, parsley, thyme, pepper, chile flakes, and salt. Let simmer for 7–8 minutes, stirring, until thickened. Remove from the heat.

2 Cook the pasta in plenty of boiling salted water until tender but still firm to the bite. Drain and return to the pan. Add the cream mixture and the cheeses to the pasta. Toss over low heat until the cheeses have melted. Transfer to a warmed serving dish.

3 Heat the oil in a large skillet over medium-high heat. Add the shrimp and scallops. Stir-fry for 2–3 minutes until the shrimp have just turned pink.

4 Pour the seafood over the pasta and toss well to mix. Sprinkle with the basil and serve at once.

pasta with scallops & pine nuts

ingredients

SERVES 4

14 oz/400 g long, hollow
   Greek macaroni or other
   short pasta
4 tbsp olive oil
1 garlic clove, chopped finely
1 oz/25 g/¼ cup pine nuts
8 large scallops, sliced
salt and pepper
2 tbsp chopped fresh basil
   leaves

method

1 Cook the macaroni in a large pan of boiling salted water for 10–12 minutes or as directed on the package, until tender.

2 About 5 minutes before the pasta is ready, heat the oil in a skillet. Add the garlic and fry for 1–2 minutes until softened but not browned. Add the pine nuts and cook until browned. Stir in the scallops and cook until just opaque. Season with salt and pepper.

3 When the pasta is cooked, drain and return to the pan. Add the scallops and the juices in the skillet to the pasta and toss together. Serve at once, sprinkled with the chopped basil.

fettuccine with scallops in porcini & cream sauce

ingredients

SERVES 4

1 oz/25 g dried porcini
   mushrooms

18 fl oz/550 ml/2¼ cups
   hot water

3 tbsp olive oil

3 tbsp butter

12 oz/350 g scallops, sliced

2 garlic cloves, chopped
   very finely

2 tbsp lemon juice

9 fl oz/250 ml/generous 1 cup
   heavy cream

salt and pepper

12 oz/350 g dried fettuccine
   or pappardelle

2 tbsp chopped fresh flat-leaf
   parsley, to serve

method

1 Put the porcini and hot water in a bowl and let soak for 20 minutes. Strain the mushrooms, reserving the soaking water, and chop coarsely. Line a strainer with paper towels and strain the mushroom water into a bowl.

2 Heat the oil and butter in a large skillet over medium heat. Add the scallops and cook for 2 minutes until just golden. Add the garlic and mushrooms and stir-fry for 1 minute.

3 Stir in the lemon juice, cream, and 4 fl oz/ 125 ml/½ cup of the mushroom water. Bring to a boil, then let simmer over medium heat for 2–3 minutes, stirring constantly, until the liquid is reduced by half. Season with salt and pepper. Remove from the heat.

4 Cook the pasta in plenty of boiling salted water until tender but still firm to the bite. Drain and transfer to a warmed serving dish. Briefly reheat the sauce and pour over the pasta. Sprinkle with the parsley and toss well to mix. Serve at once.

vegetarian

Vegetarian pasta dishes are so good that even non-vegetarians enjoy them and don't seem to notice the absence of meat!

One reason for this might be the irresistible combination of pasta, cream, and cheese that goes into some of the tastiest vegetarian recipes. If you love Parmesan cheese, try the classic Fettuccine Alfredo, which is simple but absolutely sumptuous, and Farfalle with Cream & Parmesan, which has an attractive sprinkling of bright green baby peas. If you prefer the more robust nature of Gorgonzola, which goes wonderfully with pasta, choose Pipe Rigate with Gorgonzola Sauce, Tagliatelle with Asparagus & Gorgonzola Sauce, or Fusilli with Gorgonzola & Mushroom Sauce—rich dishes for special occasions.

For everyday lunches and suppers, recipes that include plenty of vegetables are ideal. Pasta with Green Vegetables, Pasta with Spiced Leek, Butternut Squash & Cherry Tomatoes, and Penne with Bell Pepper & Goat Cheese Sauce are delicious, vibrantly colored dishes. If you favor a traditional tomato sauce, Spaghetti with Tomato, Garlic & Basil Sauce is the one for you.

Spinach, ricotta, and pasta are another perfect partnership, so we have included a recipe for Spinach & Ricotta Ravioli, using a homemade spinach pasta dough. Try it!

fettuccine alfredo

ingredients

SERVES 4

1 oz/25 g butter

7 fl oz/225 ml/scant 1 cup
  heavy cream

1 lb/450 g fresh fettuccine

1 tbsp olive oil

$3^1/4$ oz/90 g/generous $^3/4$ cup
  freshly grated Parmesan
  cheese, plus extra to serve

pinch of freshly grated nutmeg

salt and pepper

fresh flat-leaf parsley sprigs,
  to garnish

method

1 Place the butter and 5 fl oz/150 ml/$^2/3$ cup of the cream in a large pan and bring the mixture to a boil over medium heat. Reduce the heat and let simmer gently for about $1^1/2$ minutes, or until slightly thickened.

2 Meanwhile, bring a large pan of lightly salted water to a boil. Add the fettuccine and oil, return to a boil and cook for 2–3 minutes until tender but still firm to the bite. Drain the fettuccine, return it to the pan and pour the sauce over it. Return the pan to low heat and toss the fettuccine in the sauce until coated.

3 Add the remaining cream, the Parmesan cheese, and nutmeg to the fettuccine mixture and season with salt and pepper. Toss thoroughly to coat while gently heating through.

4 Transfer the fettuccine mixture to a warmed serving plate and garnish with parsley sprigs. Serve immediately, with extra grated Parmesan cheese.

paglia e fieno with garlic crumbs

ingredients

SERVES 4

12 oz/350 g/6 cups fresh
   white bread crumbs
4 tbsp finely chopped fresh
   flat-leaf parsley
1 tbsp chopped fresh chives
2 tbsp finely chopped fresh
   sweet marjoram
3 tbsp olive oil, plus extra
   to serve
3–4 garlic cloves, finely
   chopped
2 oz/55 g/1/2 cup pine nuts
salt and pepper
1 lb/450 g fresh paglia e fieno
2 oz/55 g/1/2 cup freshly
   grated romano cheese,
   to serve

method

1 Mix the bread crumbs, parsley, chives, and marjoram together in a small bowl. Heat the olive oil in a large heavy-bottom skillet. Add the bread crumb mixture and the garlic and pine nuts, season with salt and pepper, and cook over low heat, stirring constantly, for 5 minutes, or until the bread crumbs become golden, but not crisp. Remove the skillet from the heat and cover to keep warm.

2 Bring a large heavy-bottom pan of lightly salted water to a boil. Add the pasta, return to a boil, and cook for 4–5 minutes, or until tender but still firm to the bite.

3 Drain the pasta and transfer to a warmed serving dish. Drizzle with 2–3 tablespoons of olive oil and toss to mix. Add the garlic bread crumbs and toss again. Serve immediately with the grated romano cheese.

fettuccine with ricotta

ingredients

SERVES 4

12 oz/350 g dried fettuccine

3 tbsp unsalted butter

2 tbsp chopped fresh flat-leaf
   parsley, plus extra leaves
   to garnish

4 oz/115 g/generous $1/2$ cup
   ricotta cheese

4 oz/115 g/generous 1 cup
   ground almonds

5 fl oz/150 ml/$2/3$ cup
   sour cream

2 tbsp extra-virgin olive oil

4 fl oz/125 ml/$1/2$ cup hot
   chicken stock

pinch of freshly grated nutmeg

salt and pepper

1 tbsp pine nuts

method

1 Bring a large heavy-bottom pan of lightly salted water to a boil. Add the pasta, return to a boil, and cook for 8–10 minutes, or until tender but still firm to the bite. Drain well and return to the pan. Add the butter and chopped parsley and toss thoroughly to coat.

2 Mix the ricotta, ground almonds, and sour cream together in a bowl. Gradually stir in the olive oil, followed by the hot chicken stock. Season with nutmeg and pepper.

3 Transfer the pasta to a warmed dish, pour over the sauce, and toss. Sprinkle with pine nuts, garnish with parsley leaves, and serve immediately.

pasta with pesto

ingredients

SERVES 4

1 lb/450 g dried tagliatelle

salt

fresh basil sprigs, to garnish

pesto

2 garlic cloves

1 oz/25 g/$\frac{1}{4}$ cup pine nuts

salt

4 oz/115 g fresh basil leaves

2 oz/55 g/$\frac{1}{2}$ cup freshly
  grated Parmesan cheese

4 fl oz/125 ml/$\frac{1}{2}$ cup olive oil

method

1 To make the pesto, put the garlic, pine nuts, a large pinch of salt, and the basil into a mortar and pound to a paste with a pestle. Transfer to a bowl and gradually, with a wooden spoon, work in the Parmesan cheese followed by the olive oil, to make a thick, creamy sauce. Taste and adjust the seasoning if necessary.

2 Alternatively, put the garlic, pine nuts, and a large pinch of salt into a food processor or blender and process briefly. Add the basil leaves and process to a paste. With the motor still running, gradually add the olive oil. Scrape into a bowl and beat in the Parmesan cheese. Season with salt.

3 Bring a large pan of lightly salted water to a boil. Add the pasta, return to a boil, and cook for 8–10 minutes, or until tender but still firm to the bite. Drain the pasta well, return to the pan, and toss with half the pesto, then divide among warmed serving plates and top with the remaining pesto. Garnish with basil sprigs and serve immediately.

spaghetti olio e aglio

ingredients

SERVES 4

1 lb/450 g dried spaghetti

4 fl oz/125 ml/¹/₂ cup extra-
   virgin olive oil

3 garlic cloves, finely chopped

salt and pepper

3 tbsp chopped fresh flat-leaf
   parsley

method

1 Bring a large, heavy-bottom pan of lightly salted water to a boil. Add the spaghetti, return to a boil, and cook for 8–10 minutes, or until tender but still firm to the bite.

2 Meanwhile, heat the olive oil in a heavy-bottom skillet. Add the garlic and a pinch of salt and cook over low heat, stirring constantly, for 3–4 minutes, or until golden. Do not allow the garlic to brown or it will taste bitter. Remove the skillet from the heat.

3 Drain the pasta and transfer to a warmed serving dish. Pour in the garlic-flavored olive oil, then add the chopped parsley and season with salt and pepper. Toss well and serve immediately.

farfalle with cream & parmesan

ingredients

SERVES 4

1 lb/450 g dried farfalle

2 tbsp unsalted butter

12 oz/350 g/3 cups baby peas

7 fl oz/200 ml/generous $^3/_4$ cup heavy cream

pinch of freshly grated nutmeg

salt and pepper

2 oz/55 g/$^1/_2$ cup freshly grated Parmesan cheese, plus extra to serve

fresh flat-leaf parsley sprigs, to garnish

crusty bread, to serve

method

1 Bring a large pan of lightly salted water to a boil. Add the pasta, return to a boil, and cook for 8–10 minutes, or until tender but still firm to the bite, then drain thoroughly.

2 Melt the butter in a large, heavy-bottom pan. Add the baby peas and cook for 2–3 minutes. Add 5 fl oz/150 ml/$^2/_3$ cup of the cream and bring to a boil. Reduce the heat and simmer for 1 minute, or until slightly thickened.

3 Add the drained pasta to the cream mixture. Place the pan over low heat and toss until the farfalle are thoroughly coated. Season with nutmeg, salt, and pepper, then add the remaining cream and the grated Parmesan cheese. Toss again and transfer to individual serving bowls. Garnish with parsley sprigs and serve immediately with extra Parmesan cheese, for sprinkling, and crusty bread.

pipe rigate with gorgonzola sauce

ingredients

SERVES 4

14 oz/400 g dried pipe rigate,
    rigatoni, or penne
2 tbsp unsalted butter
6 fresh sage leaves
7 oz/200 g Gorgonzola cheese,
    diced
6–8 fl oz/175–225 ml/
    3/4–1 cup heavy cream
2 tbsp dry vermouth
salt and pepper

method

1 Bring a large heavy-bottom pan of lightly salted water to a boil. Add the pasta, return to a boil, and cook for 8–10 minutes, until tender but still firm to the bite.

2 Meanwhile, melt the butter in a separate heavy-bottom pan. Add the sage leaves and cook, stirring gently, for 1 minute. Remove and reserve the sage leaves. Add the cheese and cook, stirring constantly, over low heat until it has melted. Gradually, stir in 6 fl oz/ 175 ml/3/4 cup of the cream and the vermouth. Season with salt and pepper and cook, stirring, until thickened. Add more cream if the sauce seems too thick.

3 Drain the pasta well and transfer to a warmed serving dish. Add the Gorgonzola sauce, toss well to mix, and serve at once, garnished with the reserved sage leaves.

pasta with green vegetables

ingredients

SERVES 4

8 oz/225 g dried gemelli or
    other pasta shapes
2 tbsp chopped fresh parsley
2 tbsp freshly grated
    Parmesan cheese

sauce

1 head of broccoli,
    cut into florets
2 zucchini, sliced
8 oz/225 g asparagus,
    trimmed
$4^1/_2$ oz/125 g snow peas
$4^1/_2$ oz/125 g frozen peas
1 oz/25 g butter
3 tbsp vegetable stock
5 tbsp heavy cream
salt and pepper
large pinch of freshly grated
    nutmeg

method

1 Bring a large, heavy-bottom pan of lightly salted water to a boil. Add the pasta, return to a boil, and cook for 8–10 minutes, or until tender but still firm to the bite. Drain the pasta, return to the pan, cover, and keep warm.

2 Steam the broccoli, zucchini, asparagus, and snow peas over a pan of boiling, salted water until just beginning to soften. Remove from the heat and plunge into cold water to prevent further cooking. Drain and reserve. Cook the peas in boiling, salted water for 3 minutes, then drain. Refresh in cold water and drain again.

3 Place the butter and vegetable stock in a pan over medium heat. Add all the vegetables except for the asparagus and toss carefully with a wooden spoon to heat through, taking care not to break them up. Stir in the cream, let the sauce heat through, and season with salt, pepper, and nutmeg.

4 Transfer the pasta to a warmed serving dish and stir in the chopped parsley. Spoon the sauce over, and sprinkle on the freshly grated Parmesan cheese. Arrange the asparagus in a pattern on top. Serve immediately.

tagliatelle with asparagus & gorgonzola sauce

ingredients

SERVES 4

1 lb/450 g asparagus tips

olive oil

salt and pepper

8 oz/225 g Gorgonzola, crumbled

6 fl oz/175 ml/¾ cup heavy cream

12 oz/350 g dried tagliatelle

method

1 Place the asparagus tips in a single layer in a shallow ovenproof dish. Sprinkle with a little olive oil and season with salt and pepper. Turn to coat in the oil and seasoning. Roast in a preheated oven, 450°F/230°C, for 10–12 minutes until slightly browned and just tender. Set aside and keep warm.

2 Combine the crumbled cheese with the cream in a bowl. Season with salt and pepper.

3 Cook the pasta in plenty of boiling salted water until tender but still firm to the bite. Drain and transfer to a warmed serving dish.

4 Immediately add the asparagus and the cheese mixture. Toss well until the cheese has melted and the pasta is coated with the sauce. Serve at once.

radiatore with pumpkin sauce

ingredients

SERVES 4

4 tbsp unsalted butter

4 oz/115 g white onions or
   shallots, very finely chopped

1 lb 12 oz/800 g pumpkin,
   unprepared weight

pinch of freshly grated nutmeg

12 oz/350 g dried radiatore

7 fl oz/200 ml/generous
   $3/4$ cup light cream

4 tbsp freshly grated
   Parmesan cheese,
   plus extra to serve

2 tbsp chopped fresh flat-leaf
   parsley

salt and pepper

method

1 Melt the butter in a heavy-bottom pan over low heat. Add the onions, sprinkle with a little salt, cover, and cook, stirring frequently, for 25–30 minutes.

2 Scoop out and discard the seeds from the pumpkin. Peel and finely chop the flesh. Tip the pumpkin into the pan and season with nutmeg. Cover and cook over low heat, stirring occasionally, for 45 minutes.

3 Meanwhile, bring a large pan of lightly salted water to a boil. Add the pasta, return to a boil, and cook for 8–10 minutes, or until tender but still firm to the bite. Drain thoroughly, reserving about 5 fl oz/150 ml/$2/3$ cup of the cooking liquid.

4 Stir the cream, grated Parmesan cheese, and parsley into the pumpkin sauce and season with salt and pepper. If the mixture seems too thick, add some or all of the reserved cooking liquid and stir. Tip in the pasta and toss for 1 minute. Serve at once, with extra Parmesan cheese for sprinkling.

pasta with spiced leek, butternut squash & cherry tomatoes

ingredients

SERVES 4

$5^1/_2$ oz/150 g baby leeks, cut
   into $^3/_4$-inch/2-cm slices
6 oz/175 g butternut squash,
   seeded and cut into
   $^3/_4$-inch/2-cm chunks
$1^1/_2$ tbsp medium curry paste
1 tsp vegetable oil
6 oz/175 g cherry tomatoes
9 oz/250 g dried pasta
   shapes
2 tbsp chopped fresh cilantro
   leaves

white sauce

9 fl oz/250 ml/generous 1 cup
   skim milk
$^3/_4$ oz/20 g cornstarch
1 tsp mustard powder
1 small onion, left whole
2 small bay leaves
4 tsp grated Parmesan
   cheese

method

1 To make the white sauce, put the milk into a small pan with the flour, mustard, onion, and bay leaves. Whisk over medium heat until thick. Remove from the heat, discard the onion and bay leaves, and stir in the cheese. Set aside, stirring occasionally to prevent a skin forming.

2 Bring a large pan of water to a boil, add the leeks and cook for 2 minutes. Add the butternut squash and cook for a further 2 minutes. Drain in a colander.

3 Mix the curry paste with the oil in a large bowl. Toss the leeks and butternut squash in the mixture to coat thoroughly.

4 Transfer the leeks and butternut squash to a nonstick cookie sheet and roast in a preheated oven, 400°F/200°C, for 10 minutes until golden brown. Add the tomatoes and roast for a further 5 minutes.

5 Meanwhile, cook the pasta according to the instructions on the package and drain.

6 Put the white sauce into a large pan and warm over low heat. Add the leeks, butternut squash, tomatoes, and cilantro and stir in the warm pasta. Mix thoroughly and serve.

spaghetti with tomato, garlic & basil sauce

ingredients

SERVES 4

5 tbsp extra-virgin olive oil

1 onion, chopped finely

1 lb 12 oz/800 g canned
chopped tomatoes

4 garlic cloves, cut into
fourths

salt and pepper

1 lb/450 g dried spaghetti

large handful fresh basil
leaves, shredded

fresh Parmesan cheese
shavings, to serve

method

1 Heat the oil in a large pan over medium heat. Add the onion and fry gently for 5 minutes until soft. Add the tomatoes and garlic. Bring to a boil, then let simmer over medium-low heat for 25–30 minutes until the oil separates from the tomato. Season with salt and pepper.

2 Cook the pasta in plenty of boiling salted water until tender but still firm to the bite. Drain and transfer to a warmed serving dish.

3 Pour the sauce over the pasta. Add the basil and toss well to mix. Serve with the Parmesan cheese shavings.

fusilli with herbed sun-dried tomato sauce

ingredients

SERVES 4

3 oz/85 g sun-dried tomatoes
(not in oil)

24 fl oz/750 ml/3 cups boiling
water

2 tbsp olive oil

1 onion, chopped finely

2 large garlic cloves, sliced
finely

2 tbsp chopped fresh flat-leaf
parsley

2 tsp chopped fresh oregano

1 tsp chopped fresh rosemary

salt and pepper

12 oz/350 g dried fusilli

10 fresh basil leaves,
shredded and 3 tbsp
freshly grated Parmesan
cheese, to serve

method

1 Put the tomatoes and boiling water in a bowl and let stand for 5 minutes. Using a perforated spoon, remove one third of the tomatoes from the bowl. Cut into bite-size pieces. Put the remaining tomatoes and water into a blender and purée.

2 Heat the oil in a large skillet over medium heat. Add the onion and gently fry for 5 minutes until soft. Add the garlic and fry until just beginning to color. Add the puréed tomato and the reserved tomato pieces to the pan. Bring to a boil, then let simmer over medium-low heat for 10 minutes. Stir in the herbs and season with salt and pepper. Let simmer for 1 minute, then remove from the heat.

3 Cook the pasta in plenty of boiling salted water, until tender but still firm to the bite. Drain and transfer to a warmed serving dish. Briefly reheat the sauce. Pour over the pasta, add the basil and toss well to mix. Sprinkle with the Parmesan cheese and serve immediately.

hot chile pasta

ingredients

SERVES 4

5 fl oz/150 ml/$^2/_3$ cup dry
 white wine
1 tbsp sun-dried tomato paste
2 fresh red chiles
2 garlic cloves, finely chopped
12 oz/350 g dried tortiglioni
4 tbsp chopped fresh flat-leaf
 parsley
fresh romano cheese
 shavings, to garnish

sugocasa
5 tbsp extra-virgin olive oil
1 lb/450 g plum tomatoes,
 chopped
salt and pepper

method

1 First make the sugocasa. Heat the olive oil in a skillet until it is almost smoking. Add the tomatoes and cook over high heat for 2–3 minutes. Reduce the heat to low and cook gently for 20 minutes, or until very soft. Season with salt and pepper, then pass through a food mill or blender into a clean pan.

2 Add the wine, sun-dried tomato paste, whole chiles, and garlic to the sugocasa and bring to a boil. Reduce the heat and simmer gently.

3 Meanwhile, bring a large pan of lightly salted water to a boil. Add the pasta, return to a boil, and cook for 8–10 minutes, or until tender but still firm to the bite.

4 Meanwhile, remove the chiles and taste the sauce. If you prefer a hotter flavor, chop some or all of the chiles and return them to the pan. Check the seasoning at the same time, then stir in half the parsley.

5 Drain the pasta and tip it into a warmed serving bowl. Add the sauce and toss to coat. Sprinkle with the remaining parsley, garnish with the romano shavings, and serve at once.

chile broccoli pasta

ingredients

SERVES 4

8 oz/225 g dried penne or
macaroni

8 oz/225 g head of broccoli,
cut into florets

2 fl oz/50 ml/$^1/_4$ cup extra-
virgin olive oil

2 large garlic cloves, chopped

2 fresh red chiles, seeded
and diced

8 cherry tomatoes (optional)

fresh basil leaves, to garnish

method

1 Bring a large pan of salted boiling water to a boil. Add the pasta, return to a boil, and cook for 8–10 minutes until tender but still firm to the bite. Drain the pasta, refresh under cold running water, and drain again. Set aside.

2 Bring a separate pan of salted water to a boil, add the broccoli, and cook for 5 minutes. Drain, refresh under cold running water, and drain again.

3 Heat the oil in the pan that the pasta was cooked in over high heat. Add the garlic, chiles, and tomatoes, if using, and cook, stirring, for 1 minute.

4 Add the broccoli and mix well. Cook for 2 minutes, stirring, to heat through. Add the pasta and mix well again. Cook for an additional minute. Transfer the pasta to a large, warmed serving bowl and serve garnished with basil leaves.

penne in a creamy mushroom sauce

ingredients

SERVES 4

2 oz/55 g butter

1 tbsp olive oil

6 shallots, sliced

1 lb/450 g chestnut
    mushrooms, sliced

salt and pepper

1 tsp plain flour

5 fl oz/150 ml/^{2}/$_3$ cup
    heavy cream

2 tbsp port

4 oz/115 g sun-dried
    tomatoes in oil, drained
    and chopped

pinch freshly grated nutmeg

12 oz/350 g dried penne

2 tbsp chopped fresh flat-leaf
    parsley

method

1 Melt the butter with the olive oil in a large, heavy-bottom skillet. Add the shallots and cook over low heat, stirring occasionally, for 4–5 minutes, or until softened. Add the mushrooms and cook over low heat for a further 2 minutes. Season with salt and pepper, sprinkle in the flour and cook, stirring, for 1 minute.

2 Remove the skillet from the heat and gradually stir in the cream and port. Return to the heat, add the sun-dried tomatoes and grated nutmeg, and cook over low heat, stirring occasionally, for 8 minutes.

3 Meanwhile, bring a large, heavy-bottom pan of lightly salted water to a boil. Add the pasta, return to a boil and cook for 8–10 minutes, or until tender but still firm to the bite. Drain the pasta well and add to the mushroom sauce. Cook for 3 minutes, then transfer to a warmed serving dish. Sprinkle with the chopped parsley and serve immediately.

fusilli with gorgonzola & mushroom sauce

ingredients

SERVES 4

12 oz/350 g dried fusilli

3 tbsp olive oil

12 oz/350 g wild mushrooms
or white mushrooms, sliced

1 garlic clove, finely chopped

14 fl oz/400 ml/1³/₄ cups
heavy cream

9 oz/250 g Gorgonzola cheese,
crumbled

salt and pepper

2 tbsp chopped fresh flat-leaf
parsley, to garnish

method

1 Bring a large pan of lightly salted water to a boil. Add the pasta, return to a boil, and cook for 8–10 minutes, or until tender but still firm to the bite.

2 Meanwhile, heat the olive oil in a heavy-bottom pan. Add the mushrooms and cook over low heat, stirring frequently, for 5 minutes. Add the garlic to the pan and cook for an additional 2 minutes.

3 Add the cream, bring to a boil, and cook for 1 minute, until slightly thickened. Stir in the cheese and cook over low heat until it has melted. Do not allow the sauce to boil once the cheese has been added. Season with salt and pepper and remove the pan from the heat.

4 Drain the pasta and tip it into the sauce. Toss well to coat, then serve immediately, garnished with the parsley.

tagliatelle with roasted artichokes & horseradish-herb sauce

ingredients

SERVES 2

$3^1/_2$ oz/100 g canned
   artichokes, cut into
   quarters
vegetable oil spray
$1^3/_4$ oz/50 g fresh baby
   spinach leaves
$3^1/_2$ oz/100 g dried tagliatelle
$3^1/_2$ fl oz/100 ml white sauce
   (see page 162)
2 tsp chopped fresh basil,
   plus extra to garnish
1 tsp finely chopped fresh
   lemon thyme, plus extra
   to garnish
1 tsp creamed horseradish
2 tsp sour cream

method

1 Spread the artichokes out on a nonstick cookie sheet, spray lightly with oil, and roast in a preheated oven, 425°F/220°C, for 20 minutes until golden brown.

2 Meanwhile, heat a large, lidded pan over medium heat. Add the spinach, cover, and steam for 2 minutes. Remove from the heat and drain the spinach in a colander.

3 Cook the pasta according to the instructions on the package and drain.

4 Return the drained spinach to the pan, add the sauce and heat gently. Add the herbs, horseradish, sour cream, and artichokes and stir in the warm pasta. Heat to warm through, then serve garnished with extra herbs.

conchiglie with marinated artichoke, onion & tomato sauce

ingredients

SERVES 4

10 oz/280 g bottled
    marinated artichoke hearts

3 tbsp olive oil

1 onion, chopped finely

3 garlic cloves, minced

1 tsp dried oregano

$1/4$ tsp dried chile flakes

14 oz/400 g canned chopped
    tomatoes

salt and pepper

12 oz/350 g dried conchiglie

4 tsp freshly grated Parmesan
    cheese

3 tbsp chopped fresh flat-leaf
    parsley

method

1 Drain the artichoke hearts, reserving the marinade. Heat the oil in a large pan over medium heat. Add the onion and fry for 5 minutes until translucent. Add the garlic, oregano, chile flakes, and the reserved artichoke marinade. Cook for an additional 5 minutes.

2 Stir in the tomatoes. Bring to a boil, then simmer over medium-low heat for 30 minutes. Season generously with salt and pepper.

3 Cook the pasta in plenty of boiling salted water until tender but still firm to the bite. Drain and transfer to a warmed serving dish.

4 Add the artichokes, Parmesan cheese, and parsley to the sauce. Cook for a few minutes until heated through. Pour the sauce over the pasta, toss well to mix, and serve at once.

fusilli with zucchini, lemon & rosemary sauce

ingredients

SERVES 4

6 tbsp olive oil

1 small onion, sliced very thinly

2 garlic cloves, chopped very finely

2 tbsp chopped fresh rosemary

1 tbsp chopped fresh flat-leaf parsley

1 lb/450 g small zucchini, cut into $1/4$-inch x $1^{1}/2$-inch/ 5-mm x 4-cm strips

finely grated rind of 1 lemon

salt and pepper

1 lb/450 g fusilli tricolore

4 tbsp freshly grated Parmesan cheese

method

1 Heat the olive oil in a large skillet over medium-low heat. Add the onion and gently fry, stirring occasionally, for about 10 minutes until golden.

2 Raise the heat to medium-high. Add the garlic, rosemary, and parsley and cook for a few seconds, stirring. Add the zucchini and lemon rind. Cook for 5–7 minutes, stirring occasionally, until the zucchini are just tender. Season with salt and pepper. Remove from the heat.

3 Cook the pasta in plenty of boiling salted water until tender but still firm to the bite. Drain and transfer to a warmed serving dish.

4 Briefly reheat the zucchini. Pour over the pasta and toss well to mix. Sprinkle with the Parmesan cheese and serve immediately.

eggplant & pasta

ingredients

SERVES 4

5 fl oz/150 ml/^{2}/3 cup
    vegetable stock
5 fl oz/150 ml/^{2}/3 cup white
    wine vinegar
2 tsp balsamic vinegar
3 tbsp olive oil
1 fresh oregano sprig
1 lb/450 g eggplants, peeled
    and thinly sliced
14 oz/400 g dried linguine

marinade

2 tbsp extra-virgin olive oil
2 garlic cloves, crushed
2 tbsp chopped fresh oregano
2 tbsp finely chopped roasted
    almonds
2 tbsp diced red bell pepper
2 tbsp lime juice
grated rind and juice
    of 1 orange
salt and pepper

method

1 Place the vegetable stock, wine vinegar, and balsamic vinegar into a large, heavy-bottom pan and bring to a boil over low heat. Add 2 teaspoons of the olive oil and the oregano sprig, and let simmer gently for 1 minute. Add the eggplant slices to the pan, remove from the heat and let stand for 10 minutes.

2 Meanwhile, make the marinade. Mix the olive oil, garlic, fresh oregano, almonds, bell pepper, lime juice, and orange rind and juice together in a large bowl, and season with salt and pepper.

3 Carefully remove the eggplant from the pan with a slotted spoon, and drain well. Add the eggplant slices to the marinade, mixing well, and let marinate in the refrigerator for 12 hours.

4 Bring a large, heavy-bottom pan of lightly salted water to a boil. Add half of the remaining olive oil and the linguine, return to a boil, and cook for 8–10 minutes, or until just tender but still firm to the bite. Drain the pasta thoroughly and toss with the remaining olive oil while still warm. Arrange the pasta on a serving plate with the eggplant slices and the marinade. Serve immediately.

tagliatelle with walnuts

ingredients

SERVES 4

1 oz/25 g/$^1/_2$ cup fresh white
   bread crumbs

12 oz/350 g/3 cups walnut
   pieces

2 garlic cloves, finely chopped

4 tbsp milk

4 tbsp olive oil

3 oz/85 g/$^3/_8$ cup cream
   cheese

5 fl oz/150 ml/$^2/_3$ cup light
   cream

salt and pepper

12 oz/350 g dried tagliatelle

method

1 Place the bread crumbs, walnuts, garlic, milk, olive oil, and cream cheese in a large mortar and grind to a smooth paste with a pestle. Alternatively, place the ingredients in a food processor and process until smooth. Stir in the cream to give a thick sauce consistency and season with salt and pepper. Set aside.

2 Bring a large heavy-bottom pan of lightly salted water to a boil. Add the pasta, return to a boil, and cook for 8–10 minutes, or until tender but still firm to the bite.

3 Drain the pasta and transfer to a warmed serving dish. Add the walnut sauce and toss thoroughly to coat. Serve immediately.

ziti with arugula

ingredients

SERVES 4

12 oz/350 g dried ziti, broken
    into 1$^1/_2$-inch/4-cm lengths

5 tbsp extra-virgin olive oil

2 garlic cloves, lightly crushed

7 oz/200 g arugula

2 fresh red chiles,
    thickly sliced

fresh red chile flowers,
    to garnish

freshly grated romano cheese,
    to serve

method

1 Bring a large, heavy-bottom pan of lightly salted water to a boil. Add the pasta, return to a boil, and cook for 8–10 minutes, or until tender but still firm to the bite.

2 Meanwhile, heat the olive oil in a large, heavy-bottom skillet. Add the garlic, arugula, and chiles and stir-fry for 5 minutes, or until the arugula has wilted.

3 Stir 2 tablespoons of the pasta cooking water into the arugula, then drain the pasta and add to the skillet. Cook, stirring frequently, for 2 minutes, then transfer to a warmed serving dish. Remove and discard the garlic cloves and chiles, garnish with red chile flowers, and serve immediately with the romano cheese.

pasta provençal

ingredients

SERVES 4

8 oz/225 g dried penne

1 tbsp olive oil

salt and pepper

1 oz/25 g pitted black olives, drained and chopped

1 oz/25 g dry-pack sun-dried tomatoes, soaked, strained, and chopped

14 oz/400 g canned artichoke hearts, strained and halved

4 oz/115 g baby zucchini, trimmed and sliced

4 oz/115 g baby plum tomatoes, halved

3$^{1}/_{2}$ oz/100 g assorted baby salad leaves

shredded basil leaves, to garnish

dressing

4 tbsp canned crushed tomatoes

2 tbsp lowfat cream cheese

1 tbsp unsweetened orange juice

1 small bunch of fresh basil, shredded

method

1 Cook the pasta according to the package instructions, or until tender but still firm to the bite. Drain well and return to the pan. Stir in the oil, salt, pepper, olives, and sun-dried tomatoes. Set aside to cool.

2 Gently mix the artichokes, zucchini, and plum tomatoes into the cooked pasta.

3 To make the dressing, mix all the ingredients together and toss into the vegetables and pasta.

4 Arrange the salad leaves in a large serving bowl. Spoon the mixture on top of the salad leaves and garnish with shredded basil leaves.

linguine with roasted garlic & red bell pepper sauce

ingredients

SERVES 4

6 large garlic cloves,
   unpeeled

14 oz/400 g bottled roasted
   red bell peppers, strained
   and sliced

7 oz/200 g canned chopped
   tomatoes

3 tbsp olive oil

$1/4$ tsp dried chile flakes

1 tsp chopped fresh thyme or
   oregano

salt and pepper

12 oz/350 g dried linguine,
   spaghetti, or bucatini

freshly grated Parmesan
   cheese, to serve

method

1 Place the unpeeled garlic cloves in a shallow, ovenproof dish. Roast in a preheated oven at 400°F/200°C for 7–10 minutes until the cloves feel soft.

2 Put the bell peppers, tomatoes, and oil in a food processor or blender, then purée. Squeeze the garlic flesh into the purée. Add the chile flakes and oregano. Season with salt and pepper. Blend again, then scrape into a pan and set aside.

3 Cook the pasta in plenty of boiling salted water until tender but still firm to the bite. Drain and transfer to a warmed serving dish.

4 Reheat the sauce and pour over the pasta. Toss well to mix. Serve at once with Parmesan cheese.

penne with bell pepper & goat cheese sauce

ingredients

SERVES 4

2 tbsp olive oil

1 tbsp butter

1 small onion, chopped finely

4 bell peppers, yellow and
   red, seeded and cut into
   $^3/_4$-inch/2-cm squares

3 garlic cloves, sliced thinly

salt and pepper

1 lb/450 g dried penne or
   rigatoni

$4^1/_2$ oz/125 g goat cheese,
   crumbled

15 fresh basil leaves, shredded

10 black olives, pitted
   and sliced

method

1 Heat the oil and butter in a large skillet over medium heat. Add the onion and fry until soft. Raise the heat to medium-high and add the bell peppers and garlic. Cook for 12–15 minutes, stirring, until the bell peppers are just tender. Season with salt and pepper. Remove from the heat.

2 Cook the pasta in plenty of boiling salted water until tender but still firm to the bite. Drain and transfer to a warmed serving dish. Add the goat cheese and toss to mix.

3 Briefly reheat the sauce. Add the basil and olives. Pour over the pasta and toss well to mix, then serve immediately.

spinach & ricotta ravioli

ingredients

SERVES 4

spinach pasta
dough

8 oz/225 g spinach leaves

7 oz/200 g/1 cup all-purpose
  flour, plus extra for dusting

pinch of salt

2 eggs, lightly beaten

1 tbsp olive oil

filling

12 oz/350 g spinach leaves,
  coarse stalks removed

8 oz/225 g/1 cup ricotta
  cheese

2 oz/55 g/^{1}/$_2$ cup freshly
  grated Parmesan cheese,
  plus extra, to serve

2 eggs, lightly beaten

pinch of freshly grated nutmeg

pepper

all-purpose flour, for dusting

method

1 To make the pasta dough, blanch the spinach in boiling water for 1 minute, then drain thoroughly and chop finely. Sift the flour into a food processor. Add the spinach, salt, eggs, and olive oil and process until the dough begins to come together. Knead on a lightly floured counter until smooth. Cover and let rest for 30 minutes.

2 To make the filling, cook the spinach, with just the water clinging to the leaves after washing, over low heat for 5 minutes, or until wilted. Drain and squeeze out as much moisture as possible. Cool, then chop finely. Beat the ricotta cheese until smooth, then stir in the spinach, Parmesan cheese, and half the egg, and season with nutmeg and pepper.

3 Halve the pasta dough. Roll out one half on a floured counter. Cover, and roll out the other half. Put small mounds of filling in rows 1^1/$_2$ inches/4 cm apart on one sheet of dough and brush in between with the remaining egg. Cover with the other half. Press down between the mounds, pushing out any air. Cut into squares and let rest on a dish towel for 1 hour.

4 Bring a large pan of salted water to a boil, add the ravioli, in batches, return to a boil, and cook for 5 minutes. Remove with a slotted spoon and drain on paper towels. Serve with grated Parmesan cheese.

al forno
(baked in the oven)

It's cold, it's wet, you're feeling miserable, and you need cheering up—fast! A baked pasta dish is the answer. Layers of pasta and sauce with a cheese topping, pasta tubes stuffed with a delicious filling, or the ultimate comfort food, Macaroni & Cheese, will chase away those blues. Resist the temptation to open the oven door while your favorite recipe is cooking—instead, enjoy the anticipation of that tastebud-tempting aroma as the finished dish emerges, piping hot and bubbling on top.

Lasagne are among the best-loved pasta dishes—try a traditional Lasagna or Lasagna Verde, a Chicken Lasagna, or a Marsala Mushroom Lasagna. For a seafood version, Lasagna alla Marinara is packed with shrimp and monkfish, while Vegetarian Lasagna is layered with a tantalizing mix of charbroilled eggplants and zucchini fried with garlic and herbs.

Cannelloni is fun to make—large tubes of pasta stuffed with your favorite filling and baked in a sauce. Try Chicken & Wild Mushroom Cannelloni, or Cannelloni with Spinach & Ricotta. Mixed Vegetable Agnolotti are stuffed half-circles of homemade pasta, cooked first in boiling water then finished off in the oven with a generous coating of Parmesan cheese. It comes with a feel-good guarantee!

lasagna verde

ingredients

SERVES 4

butter, for greasing

8 oz/225 g no-precook
   lasagna verde

10 fl oz/300 ml/1¹/₄ cups
   béchamel sauce
   (see page 230)

2 oz/55 g/¹/₂ cup freshly
   grated Parmesan cheese

green salad, tomato salad, or
   black olives, to serve

meat sauce

3 tbsp olive oil

1¹/₂ oz/45 g butter

2 large onions, chopped

4 celery stalks, thinly sliced

6 oz/175 g bacon, chopped

2 garlic cloves, chopped

1 lb 2 oz/500 g fresh
   ground beef

2 tbsp tomato paste

1 tbsp all-purpose flour

14 oz/400 g canned chopped
   tomatoes

5 fl oz/150 ml/²/₃ cup beef
   stock

5 fl oz/150 ml/²/₃ cup red wine

salt and pepper

2 tsp dried oregano

¹/₂ tsp freshly grated nutmeg

method

1 To make the meat sauce, heat the oil and butter in a large skillet over medium heat. Add the onions, celery, and bacon and fry for 5 minutes, stirring. Stir in the garlic and ground beef and cook, stirring, until the meat changes color. Reduce the heat and cook for 10 minutes, stirring.

2 Increase the heat to medium, stir in the tomato paste and the flour, and cook for 1–2 minutes. Stir in the tomatoes, stock, and wine and bring to a boil, stirring. Season with salt and pepper and stir in the oregano and nutmeg. Let simmer uncovered, stirring, for 55 minutes–1 hour, or until the mixture is reduced to a thick paste.

3 Spoon a little of the meat sauce into a greased rectangular ovenproof dish, cover with a layer of lasagna, then spoon over a little béchamel sauce. Continue making layers in this way, covering the final layer of lasagne with the remaining béchamel sauce.

4 Sprinkle over the cheese and bake in a preheated oven, 375°F/190°C, for 40 minutes, or until the sauce is golden brown and bubbling. Serve with a green salad, a tomato salad, or a bowl of black olives.

sicilian linguine

ingredients

SERVES 4

4 fl oz/125 ml/$^1/_2$ cup olive oil,
  plus extra for brushing

2 eggplants, sliced

12 oz/350 g/1$^1/_2$ cups fresh
  ground beef

1 onion, chopped

2 garlic cloves, finely chopped

2 tbsp tomato paste

14 oz/400 g canned chopped
  tomatoes

1 tsp Worcestershire sauce

1 tbsp chopped fresh flat-leaf
  parsley

salt and pepper

2 oz/55 g/$^1/_3$ cup pitted black
  olives, sliced

1 red bell pepper, seeded
  and chopped

6 oz/175 g dried linguine

4 oz/115 g/1 cup freshly
  grated Parmesan cheese

method

1 Brush an 8-inch/20-cm loose-bottom round cake pan with oil and line the bottom with parchment paper. Heat half the oil in a skillet. Add the eggplants in batches, and cook until lightly browned on both sides. Add more oil, as required. Drain the eggplants on paper towels, then arrange in overlapping slices to cover the bottom and sides of the cake pan, reserving a few slices.

2 Heat the remaining olive oil in a large pan and add the beef, onion, and garlic. Cook over medium heat, breaking up the meat with a wooden spoon, until browned all over. Add the tomato paste, tomatoes and their can juices, Worcestershire sauce, and parsley. Season with salt and pepper and let simmer for 10 minutes. Add the olives and bell pepper and cook for 10 minutes.

3 Meanwhile, bring a pan of lightly salted water to a boil. Add the pasta, return to a boil, and cook for 8–10 minutes, or until tender but still firm to the bite. Drain and transfer to a bowl. Add the meat sauce and cheese and toss, then spoon into the cake pan, press down and cover with the remaining eggplant slices. Bake in a preheated oven, 400°F/200°C, for 40 minutes. Remove from the oven and let stand for 5 minutes, then loosen round the edges and invert onto a plate. Remove and discard the parchment paper and serve.

lasagna

ingredients

SERVES 4

3 tbsp olive oil

1 onion, finely chopped

1 celery stalk, finely chopped

1 carrot, finely chopped

$3^1/_2$ oz/100 g pancetta or
rindless lean bacon,
finely chopped

6 oz/175 g ground beef

6 oz/175 g ground pork

$3^1/_2$ fl oz/100 ml/generous
$^1/_3$ cup dry red wine

5 fl oz/150 ml/$^2/_3$ cup
beef stock

1 tbsp tomato paste

salt and pepper

1 clove

1 bay leaf

5 fl oz/150 ml/$^2/_3$ cup
boiling milk

4 tbsp unsalted butter, diced,
plus extra for greasing

14 oz/400 g dried
no-precook lasagna

10 fl oz/300 ml/$1^1/_4$ cups
béchamel sauce
(see page 230)

5 oz/140 g mozzarella
cheese, diced

5 oz/140 g/$1^1/_4$ cups freshly
grated Parmesan cheese

method

1 Heat the olive oil in a large, heavy-bottom pan. Add the onion, celery, carrot, pancetta, beef, and pork and cook over medium heat, stirring frequently and breaking up the meat with a wooden spoon, for 10 minutes, or until lightly browned.

2 Add the wine, bring to a boil, and cook until reduced. Add about two thirds of the stock, bring to a boil, and cook until reduced. Combine the remaining stock and tomato paste and add to the pan. Season with salt and pepper, add the clove and bay leaf, and pour in the milk. Cover and let simmer over low heat for $1^1/_2$ hours. Remove from the heat and discard the clove and bay leaf.

3 Lightly grease a large, ovenproof dish with butter. Place a layer of lasagna in the bottom and cover it with a layer of meat sauce. Spoon a layer of béchamel sauce on top and sprinkle with one third of the mozzarella and Parmesan cheeses. Continue making layers until all the ingredients are used, ending with a topping of béchamel sauce and sprinkled cheese.

4 Dot the top of the lasagna with the diced butter and bake in a preheated oven, 400°F/200°C, for 30 minutes, or until golden and bubbling.

pork & pasta casserole

ingredients

SERVES 4

2 tbsp olive oil

1 onion, chopped

1 garlic clove, finely chopped

2 carrots, diced

2 oz/55 g pancetta or rindless
    lean bacon, chopped

4 oz/115 g mushrooms,
    chopped

1 lb/450 g ground pork

4 fl oz/125 ml/$^1\!/_2$ cup
    dry white wine

4 tbsp strained canned
    tomatoes

7 oz/200 g canned chopped
    tomatoes

2 tsp chopped fresh sage or
    $^1\!/_2$ tsp dried sage

salt and pepper

8 oz/225 g dried elicoidali

5 oz/140 g mozzarella cheese,
    diced

4 tbsp freshly grated
    Parmesan cheese

$1^1\!/_4$ cups béchamel sauce
    (see page 230)

method

1 Heat the olive oil in a large, heavy-bottom skillet. Add the onion, garlic, and carrots and cook over low heat, stirring occasionally, for 5 minutes, or until the onion has softened. Add the pancetta and cook for 5 minutes. Add the chopped mushrooms and cook, stirring occasionally, for an additional 2 minutes. Add the pork and cook, breaking it up with a wooden spoon, until the meat is browned all over. Stir in the wine, strained tomatoes, chopped tomatoes and their can juices, and sage. Season with salt and pepper and bring to a boil, then cover and simmer over low heat for 25–30 minutes.

2 Meanwhile, bring a large, heavy-bottom pan of lightly salted water to a boil. Add the pasta, return to a boil, and cook for 8–10 minutes, or until tender but still firm to the bite.

3 Spoon the pork mixture into a large ovenproof dish. Stir the mozzarella and half the Parmesan cheese into the béchamel sauce. Drain the pasta and stir the sauce into it, then spoon it over the pork mixture. Sprinkle with the remaining Parmesan cheese and bake in a preheated oven, 400°F/200°C, for 25–30 minutes, or until golden brown. Serve at once.

cannelloni with ham & ricotta

ingredients

SERVES 4

2 tbsp olive oil

2 onions, chopped

2 garlic cloves, finely chopped

1 tbsp shredded fresh basil

1 lb 12 oz/800 g chopped tomatoes

1 tbsp tomato paste

salt and pepper

12 oz/350 g dried cannelloni tubes

butter, for greasing

8 oz/225 g/1 cup ricotta cheese

4 oz/115 g cooked ham, diced

1 egg

2 oz/55 g/$1/2$ cup freshly grated romano cheese

method

1 Heat the olive oil in a large, heavy-bottom skillet. Add the onions and garlic and cook over low heat, stirring occasionally, for 5 minutes, or until the onion is softened. Add the basil, chopped tomatoes and their can juices, and tomato paste and season with salt and pepper. Reduce the heat and let simmer for 30 minutes, or until thickened.

2 Meanwhile, bring a large, heavy-bottom pan of lightly salted water to a boil. Add the dried cannelloni tubes, return to a boil, and cook for 8–10 minutes, or until tender but still firm to the bite. Using a slotted spoon, transfer the cannelloni tubes to a large plate and pat dry with paper towels.

3 Grease a large, shallow ovenproof dish with butter. Mix the ricotta, ham, and egg together in a bowl and season with salt and pepper. Using a teaspoon, fill the cannelloni tubes with the ricotta, ham, and egg mixture and place in a single layer in the dish. Pour the tomato sauce over the cannelloni and sprinkle with the grated romano cheese. Bake in a preheated oven, 350°F/180°C, for 30 minutes, or until golden brown. Serve at once.

pasticcio

ingredients

SERVES 4

1 tbsp olive oil

1 onion, chopped

2 garlic cloves, finely chopped

1 lb/450 g/2 cups fresh
   ground lamb

2 tbsp tomato paste

2 tbsp all-purpose flour

10 fl oz/300 ml/1^1/$_4$ cups
   chicken stock

salt and pepper

1 tsp ground cinnamon

4 oz/115 g dried short-cut
   macaroni

2 beefsteak tomatoes, sliced

10 fl oz/300 ml/1^1/$_4$ cups
   strained plain yogurt

2 eggs, lightly beaten

method

1 Heat the olive oil in a large heavy-bottom skillet. Add the onion and garlic and cook over low heat, stirring occasionally, for 5 minutes, or until softened. Add the lamb and cook, breaking it up with a wooden spoon, until browned all over. Add the tomato paste and sprinkle in the flour. Cook, stirring, for 1 minute, then stir in the chicken stock. Season with salt and pepper and stir in the cinnamon. Bring to a boil, reduce the heat, cover, and cook for 25 minutes.

2 Meanwhile, bring a large heavy-bottom pan of lightly salted water to a boil. Add the pasta, return to a boil, and cook for 8–10 minutes, or until tender but still firm to the bite.

3 Spoon the lamb mixture into a large ovenproof dish and arrange the tomato slices on top. Drain the pasta and transfer to a bowl. Add the yogurt and eggs and mix well. Spoon the pasta mixture on top of the lamb and bake in a preheated oven, 375°F/190°C, for 1 hour. Serve immediately.

chicken cannelloni

ingredients

SERVES 4

4 skinless, boneless chicken
   breasts, diced
2 tbsp olive oil
6 tbsp butter
18 fl oz/500 ml/2^1/$_4$ cups
   heavy cream
1 tsp salt
1 tsp pepper
^{1}/$_4$ tsp freshly grated nutmeg
2 oz/55 g/^{1}/$_2$ cup freshly
   grated Parmesan cheese
1 lb/450 g/2 cups ricotta
   cheese
1 egg, lightly beaten
1 tbsp chopped fresh oregano
2 tbsp chopped fresh basil
8 oz/225 g dried cannelloni
2^3/$_4$ oz/75 g/^{2}/$_3$ cup mozzarella
   cheese, freshly grated
fresh basil sprigs, to garnish

marinade
4 fl oz/125 ml white wine
   vinegar
1 garlic clove, crushed
8 fl oz/225 ml olive oil

method

1 To make the marinade, mix the vinegar, garlic, and olive oil together in a large bowl. Add the chicken, cover with plastic wrap, and let marinate for 30 minutes.

2 Heat the 2 tablespoons of olive oil in a skillet. Drain the chicken and cook for 5–7 minutes, stirring, until it turns white. Set aside.

3 Melt the butter in a pan over medium-high heat. Add the cream, salt, pepper, and nutmeg. Stir until thickened. Reduce the heat, add the Parmesan cheese, and stir until melted. Remove from the heat.

4 Mix the ricotta, egg, and herbs together in a large bowl. Stir in the chicken then remove from the heat. Stuff the cannelloni with the chicken mixture. Pour half the sauce into a 9 x 13-inch/23 x 33-cm baking dish. Place the stuffed cannelloni on top. Pour over the remaining sauce. Sprinkle with the mozzarella and cover with foil. Bake in a preheated oven, 350°F/180°C, for 45 minutes. Let the dish stand for 10 minutes before garnishing with basil sprigs and serving.

chicken lasagna

ingredients

SERVES 6

2 tbsp olive oil

2 lb/900 g/4 cups fresh
ground chicken

1 garlic clove, finely chopped

4 carrots, chopped

4 leeks, sliced

16 fl oz/450 ml/2 cups
chicken stock

2 tbsp tomato paste

salt and pepper

4 oz/115 g Cheddar cheese,
grated

1 tsp Dijon mustard

double quantity of béchamel
sauce (see page 230)

4 oz/115 g dried no-precook
lasagna

method

1 Heat the oil in a heavy-bottom pan. Add the chicken and cook over medium heat, breaking it up with a wooden spoon, for 5 minutes, or until it is browned all over. Add the garlic, carrots, and leeks to the pan, and cook, stirring occasionally, for 5 minutes.

2 Stir in the chicken stock and tomato paste and season with salt and pepper. Bring to a boil, reduce the heat, cover, and let simmer for 30 minutes.

3 Whisk half the cheese and the mustard into the hot béchamel sauce. In a large ovenproof dish, make alternate layers of the chicken mixture, lasagna, and cheese sauce, ending with a layer of cheese sauce. Sprinkle with the remaining cheese and bake in a preheated oven, 375°F/190°C, for 1 hour, or until golden brown and bubbling. Serve at once.

marsala mushroom lasagna

ingredients

SERVES 4

butter, for greasing

14 sheets dried no-precook
  lasagna

triple quantity of béchamel
  sauce (see page 230)

3 oz/75 g/³⁄₄ cup grated
  Parmesan cheese

exotic mushroom sauce

2 tbsp olive oil

2 garlic cloves, crushed

1 large onion, finely chopped

8 oz/225 g exotic mushrooms,
  sliced

10¹⁄₂ oz/300 g/generous 1¹⁄₄
  cups fresh ground chicken

3 oz/75 g chicken livers,
  finely chopped

4 oz/115 g prosciutto, diced

5 fl oz/150 ml/²⁄₃ cup
  Marsala wine

10 oz/285 g canned chopped
  tomatoes

1 tbsp chopped fresh basil
  leaves

2 tbsp tomato paste

salt and pepper

method

1 To make the sauce, heat the olive oil in a large, heavy-bottom pan. Add the garlic, onion, and mushrooms, and cook, stirring frequently, for 6 minutes. Add the ground chicken, chicken livers, and prosciutto, and cook over low heat for 12 minutes, or until the meat has browned.

2 Stir the Marsala, tomatoes, basil, and tomato paste into the mixture, and cook for 4 minutes. Season with salt and pepper, cover, and let simmer for 30 minutes. Uncover, stir, then let simmer for an additional 15 minutes.

3 Lightly grease an ovenproof dish with butter. Arrange sheets of lasagna over the base of the dish, spoon over a layer of the exotic mushroom sauce, then spoon over a layer of béchamel sauce. Place another layer of lasagna on top and repeat the process twice, finishing with a layer of béchamel sauce. Sprinkle over the grated cheese and bake in a preheated oven, 375°F/190°C, for 35 minutes, or until golden brown and bubbling. Serve immediately.

chicken & wild mushroom cannelloni

ingredients

SERVES 4

butter, for greasing

2 tbsp olive oil

2 garlic cloves, crushed

1 large onion, finely chopped

8 oz/225 g wild mushrooms, sliced

12 oz/350 g ground chicken

115 g/4 oz prosciutto, diced

5 fl oz/150 ml/^{2}/$_3$ cup Marsala wine

7 oz/200 g canned chopped tomatoes

1 tbsp shredded fresh basil leaves

2 tbsp tomato paste

salt and pepper

10–12 dried cannelloni tubes

double quantity of béchamel sauce (see page 230)

3 oz/85 g/^{3}/$_4$ cup freshly grated Parmesan cheese

method

1 Lightly grease a large ovenproof dish. Heat the olive oil in a heavy-bottom skillet. Add the garlic, onion, and mushrooms and cook over low heat, stirring frequently, for 8–10 minutes. Add the ground chicken and prosciutto and cook, stirring frequently, for 12 minutes, or until browned all over. Stir in the Marsala, tomatoes and their can juices, basil, and tomato paste and cook for 4 minutes. Season with salt and pepper, then cover and simmer for 30 minutes. Uncover, stir, and simmer for 15 minutes.

2 Meanwhile, bring a large, heavy-bottom pan of lightly salted water to a boil. Add the pasta, return to a boil, and cook for 8–10 minutes, or until tender but still firm to the bite. Using a slotted spoon, transfer the cannelloni tubes to a plate and pat dry with paper towels.

3 Using a teaspoon, fill the cannelloni tubes with the chicken, prosciutto, and mushroom mixture. Transfer them to the ovenproof dish. Pour the béchamel sauce over them to cover completely and sprinkle with the grated Parmesan cheese.

4 Bake the cannelloni in a preheated oven, 375°F/190°C, for 30 minutes, or until golden brown and bubbling. Serve immediately.

lasagna alla marinara

ingredients

SERVES 6

1 tbsp butter

8 oz/225 g raw shrimp, shelled, deveined, and coarsely chopped

1 lb/450 g monkfish fillets, skinned and chopped

8 oz/225 g cremini mushrooms, chopped

triple quantity of béchamel sauce (see page 230)

salt and pepper

14 oz/400 g canned chopped tomatoes

1 tbsp chopped fresh chervil

1 tbsp shredded fresh basil

6 oz/175 g dried no-precook lasagna

3 oz/85 g/³⁄₄ cup freshly grated Parmesan cheese

method

1 Melt the butter in a large, heavy-bottom pan. Add the shrimp and monkfish and cook over medium heat for 3–5 minutes, or until the shrimp change color. Transfer the shrimp to a small heatproof bowl with a slotted spoon. Add the mushrooms to the pan and cook, stirring occasionally, for 5 minutes. Transfer the fish and mushrooms to the bowl.

2 Stir the fish mixture, with any juices, into the béchamel sauce and season with salt and pepper.

3 Layer the tomatoes, chervil, basil, fish mixture, and lasagna sheets in a large ovenproof dish, ending with a layer of the fish mixture. Sprinkle evenly with the grated Parmesan cheese. Bake in a preheated oven, 375°F/ 190°C, for 35 minutes, or until golden brown, then serve immediately.

baked tuna & ricotta rigatoni

ingredients

SERVES 4

1 lb/450 g dried rigatoni

4 oz/115 g sun-dried
  tomatoes in oil, drained
  and sliced

filling

7 oz/200 g canned flaked
  tuna, drained

8 oz/225 g/1 cup ricotta
  cheese

sauce

4 fl oz/125 ml/$1/2$ cup
  heavy cream

8 oz/225 g/2 cups freshly
  grated Parmesan cheese

salt and pepper

method

1 Lightly grease a large ovenproof dish with butter. Bring a large, heavy-bottom pan of lightly salted water to a boil. Add the rigatoni, return to a boil, and cook for 8–10 minutes, or until just tender but still firm to the bite. Drain the pasta and let stand until cool enough to handle.

2 Meanwhile, mix the tuna and ricotta cheese together in a bowl to form a soft paste. Spoon the mixture into a pastry bag and use to fill the rigatoni. Arrange the filled pasta tubes side by side in the prepared dish.

3 To make the sauce, mix the cream and Parmesan cheese together in a bowl and season with salt and pepper. Spoon the sauce over the rigatoni and top with the sun-dried tomatoes, arranged in a criss-cross pattern. Bake in a preheated oven, 400°F/200°C, for 20 minutes. Serve hot straight from the dish.

layered spaghetti with smoked salmon & shrimp

ingredients

SERVES 6

12 oz/350 g dried spaghetti

2$\frac{1}{2}$ oz/70 g butter, plus extra
  for greasing

7 oz/200 g smoked salmon,
  cut into strips

10 oz/280 g jumbo shrimp,
  cooked, shelled,
  and deveined

10 fl oz/300 ml/1$\frac{1}{4}$ cups
  béchamel sauce (see
  page 230)

4 oz/115 g/1 cup freshly
  grated Parmesan cheese

method

1 Bring a large pan of lightly salted water to a boil. Add the pasta, return to a boil, and cook for 8–10 minutes, or until tender but still firm to the bite. Drain well, return to the pan, add 4 tablespoons of the butter, and toss well.

2 Spoon half the spaghetti into a large, greased ovenproof dish, cover with the strips of smoked salmon, then top with the shrimp. Pour over half the béchamel sauce and sprinkle with half the Parmesan. Add the remaining spaghetti, cover with the remaining sauce, and sprinkle with the remaining Parmesan. Dice the remaining butter and dot it over the surface.

3 Bake in a preheated oven, 350°F/180°C, for 15 minutes, or until the top is golden brown. Serve immediately.

tuna noodle casserole

ingredients

SERVES 2

$4^1/_2$–$5^1/_2$ oz/125–150 g dried
   macaroni

1 tbsp olive oil

1 garlic clove, crushed

2 oz/55 g white mushrooms,
   sliced

$^1/_2$ red bell pepper, thinly sliced

7 oz/200 g canned tuna in
   spring water, drained
   and flaked

$^1/_2$ tsp dried oregano

salt and pepper

2 tomatoes, sliced

2 tbsp dried bread crumbs

1 oz/25 g/$^1/_2$ cup grated
   mature Cheddar or
   Parmesan cheese

sauce

2 tbsp butter, plus extra
   for greasing

1 tbsp all-purpose flour

9 fl oz/250 ml/1 cup milk

method

1 Bring a large pan of lightly salted water to a boil. Add the macaroni, return to a boil, and cook for 10–12 minutes, or until tender but still firm to the bite. Drain, rinse, and drain again thoroughly.

2 Heat the olive oil in a skillet and cook the garlic, mushrooms, and bell pepper until soft. Add the tuna, oregano, and salt and pepper. Heat through. Grease a 32-fl oz/1-liter/4-cup ovenproof dish with a little butter or margarine. Add half of the cooked macaroni, cover with the tuna mixture, then add the remaining macaroni.

3 To make the sauce, melt the butter in a pan, stir in the flour, and cook for 1 minute. Gradually add the milk and bring to a boil. Let simmer for 1–2 minutes, stirring constantly, until thickened. Season with salt and pepper. Pour the sauce over the macaroni. Lay the sliced tomatoes over the sauce and sprinkle with the bread crumbs and cheese. Cook in a preheated oven, 400°F/200°C, for 25 minutes, or until piping hot and the top is well browned.

shellfish casserole

ingredients

SERVES 6

12 oz/350 g dried conchiglie

6 tbsp butter, plus extra
   for greasing

2 fennel bulbs, thinly sliced

6 oz/175 g mushrooms,
   thinly sliced

6 oz/175 g cooked shelled
   shrimp

6 oz/175 g cooked crabmeat

pinch of cayenne pepper

10 fl oz/300 ml/1¼ cups
   béchamel sauce
   (see page 230)

2 oz/55 g/½ cup freshly
   grated Parmesan cheese

2 beefsteak tomatoes, sliced

olive oil, for brushing

green salad and crusty bread,
   to serve

method

1 Bring a large, heavy-bottom pan of lightly salted water to a boil. Add the pasta, return to a boil, and cook for 8–10 minutes, or until tender but still firm to the bite. Drain well, return to the pan, and stir in 2 tablespoons of the butter. Cover the pan and keep warm.

2 Meanwhile, melt the remaining butter in a large, heavy-bottom skillet. Add the fennel and cook over medium heat for 5 minutes, or until softened. Stir in the mushrooms and cook for an additional 2 minutes. Stir in the shrimp and crabmeat and cook for an additional 1 minute, then remove the skillet from the heat.

3 Grease 6 small ovenproof dishes with butter. Stir the cayenne pepper into the béchamel sauce, add the shellfish mixture and pasta, then spoon into the prepared dishes. Sprinkle with the Parmesan cheese and arrange the tomato slices on top, then brush the tomatoes with a little olive oil.

4 Bake in a preheated oven, 350°F/180°C, for 25 minutes, or until golden brown. Serve hot with a green salad and crusty bread.

macaroni & cheese

ingredients

SERVES 4

8 oz/225 g macaroni

double quantity béchamel
   sauce (see page 230)

1 egg, beaten

$4^1/_2$ oz/125 g/$1^1/_4$ cups sharp
   Cheddar cheese, grated

1 tbsp wholegrain mustard

2 tbsp chopped fresh chives

salt and pepper

4 tomatoes, sliced

$4^1/_2$ oz/125 g/$1^1/_4$ cups Red
   Leicester cheese, grated

$2^1/_4$ oz/60 g/generous $^1/_2$ cup
   bleu cheese, grated

2 tbsp sunflower seeds

snipped fresh chives,
   to garnish

method

1 Bring a large pan of lightly salted water to a boil and cook the macaroni for 8–10 minutes, or until just tender. Drain well and place in an ovenproof dish.

2 Stir the beaten egg, Cheddar cheese, mustard, and chives into the béchamel sauce and season with salt and pepper. Spoon the mixture over the macaroni, making sure it is well covered. Top with a layer of the sliced tomatoes.

3 Sprinkle the Red Leicester cheese, bleu cheese, and sunflower seeds over the top. Place on a cookie sheet and bake in a preheated oven, 375°F/190°C, for 25–30 minutes, or until bubbling and golden. Garnish with snipped fresh chives and serve at once.

vegetarian lasagna

ingredients

SERVES 4

olive oil, for brushing

2 eggplants, sliced

2 tbsp butter

1 garlic clove, finely chopped

4 zucchini, sliced

1 tbsp finely chopped fresh
flat-leaf parsley

1 tbsp finely chopped fresh
marjoram

8 oz/225 g mozzarella
cheese, grated

20 fl oz/625 ml/2¹/₂ cups
strained canned tomatoes

175 g/6 oz dried no-precook
lasagna

salt and pepper

béchamel sauce (see below)

2 oz/55 g/¹/₂ cup freshly
grated Parmesan cheese

béchamel sauce

10 fl oz/300 ml/1¹/₄ cups milk

1 bay leaf

6 black peppercorns

slice of onion

mace blade

2 tbsp butter

3 tbsp all-purpose flour

salt and pepper

method

1 To make the béchamel sauce, pour the milk into a pan and add the bay leaf, peppercorns, onion, and mace. Heat to just below boiling point, then remove from the heat, cover, let infuse for 10 minutes, and strain. Melt the butter in a separate pan. Sprinkle in the flour and cook over low heat, stirring constantly, for 1 minute. Gradually stir in the milk, then bring to a boil and cook, stirring, until thickened and smooth. Season with salt and pepper.

2 Brush a grill pan with olive oil and heat until smoking. Add half the eggplant slices and cook over medium heat for 8 minutes, or until golden brown all over. Remove from the grill pan and drain on paper towels. Repeat with the remaining eggplant slices.

3 Melt the butter in a skillet and add the garlic, zucchini, parsley, and marjoram. Cook over medium heat, stirring frequently, for 5 minutes, or until the zucchini are golden brown all over. Remove and let drain on paper towels.

4 Layer the eggplant, zucchini, mozzarella, strained tomatoes, and lasagna in an ovenproof dish brushed with olive oil, seasoning as you go and finishing with a layer of lasagna. Pour over the béchamel sauce, sprinkle with the Parmesan cheese and bake in a preheated oven, 400°F/200°C, for 30–40 minutes, or until golden brown. Serve at once.

mixed vegetable agnolotti

ingredients

SERVES 4

butter, for greasing

all-purpose flour, for dusting

3 oz/85 g/³/₄ cup freshly
grated Parmesan cheese

mixed salad greens, to serve

pasta dough

7 oz/200 g/1 cup all-purpose
flour, plus extra for dusting

pinch of salt

2 eggs, lightly beaten

1 tbsp olive oil

filling

4 fl oz/125 ml/¹/₂ cup olive oil

1 red onion, chopped

3 garlic cloves, chopped

2 large eggplants,
cut into chunks

3 large zucchini,
cut into chunks

6 beefsteak tomatoes, peeled,
seeded, and coarsely
chopped

1 large green bell pepper,
seeded and diced

1 large red bell pepper,
seeded and diced

1 tbsp sun-dried tomato paste

1 tbsp shredded fresh basil

salt and pepper

method

1 To make the pasta dough, sift the flour into a food processor. Add the salt, eggs, and olive oil and process until the dough begins to come together. Knead on a lightly floured counter until smooth. Cover and let rest for 30 minutes.

2 To make the filling, heat the olive oil in a large, heavy-bottom pan. Add the onion and garlic and cook over low heat, stirring occasionally, for 5 minutes, or until softened. Add the eggplant, zucchini, tomatoes, green and red bell peppers, sun-dried tomato paste, and basil. Season with salt and pepper, cover, and let simmer gently, stirring occasionally, for 20 minutes.

3 Lightly grease an ovenproof dish with butter. Roll out the pasta dough on a lightly floured counter and stamp out 3-inch/7.5-cm circles with a plain cutter. Place a spoonful of the vegetable filling on one side of each circle. Dampen the edges slightly and fold the pasta circles over, pressing together to seal.

4 Bring a large pan of lightly salted water to a boil. Add the agnolotti, in batches if necessary, return to a boil, and cook for 3–4 minutes. Remove with a slotted spoon, drain, and transfer to the dish. Sprinkle with the Parmesan cheese and bake in a preheated oven, 400°F/200°C, for 20 minutes. Serve with salad greens.

baked pasta with mushrooms

ingredients

SERVES 4

5 oz/140 g fontina cheese, thinly sliced

10 fl oz/300 ml/1¼ cups béchamel sauce (see page 230)

6 tbsp butter, plus extra for greasing

12 oz/350 g mixed wild mushrooms, sliced

12 oz/350 g dried tagliatelle

2 egg yolks

salt and pepper

4 tbsp freshly grated romano cheese

mixed salad greens, to serve

method

1 Stir the fontina cheese into the béchamel sauce and set aside.

2 Melt 2 tablespoons of the butter in a large pan. Add the mushrooms and cook over low heat, stirring occasionally, for 10 minutes.

3 Meanwhile, bring a large pan of lightly salted water to a boil. Add the pasta, return to a boil, and cook for 8–10 minutes, or until tender but still firm to the bite. Drain, return to the pan, and add the remaining butter, the egg yolks, and about one third of the sauce, then season with salt and pepper. Toss well to mix, then gently stir in the mushrooms.

4 Lightly grease a large, ovenproof dish with butter and spoon in the pasta mixture. Pour over the remaining sauce evenly and sprinkle with the grated romano cheese. Bake in a preheated oven, 400°F/200°C, for 15–20 minutes, or until golden brown. Serve immediately with mixed salad greens.

mushroom cannelloni

ingredients

SERVES 4

12 dried cannelloni tubes

2 tbsp butter

1 lb/450 g mixed wild
mushrooms, finely chopped

1 garlic clove, finely chopped

3 oz/85 g/1$^1/_2$ cups fresh
bread crumbs

5 fl oz/150 ml/$^2/_3$ cup milk

4 tbsp olive oil, plus extra
for brushing

8 oz/225 g/1 cup ricotta
cheese

6 tbsp freshly grated
Parmesan cheese

salt and pepper

2 tbsp pine nuts

2 tbsp slivered almonds

tomato sauce

2 tbsp olive oil

1 onion, finely chopped

1 garlic clove, finely chopped

1 lb 12 oz/800 g canned
chopped tomatoes

1 tbsp tomato paste

8 black olives, pitted
and chopped

salt and pepper

method

1 Bring a large pan of lightly salted water to a boil. Add the cannelloni tubes, return to a boil, and cook for 8–10 minutes, or until tender but still firm to the bite. With a slotted spoon, transfer the tubes to a plate and pat dry.

2 Meanwhile, make the tomato sauce. Heat the olive oil in a skillet. Add the onion and garlic and cook over low heat for 5 minutes, or until softened. Add the tomatoes and their can juices, tomato paste, and olives and season with salt and pepper. Bring to a boil and cook for 3–4 minutes. Pour the sauce into an large ovenproof dish brushed with olive oil.

3 To make the filling, melt the butter in a heavy-bottom skillet. Add the mushrooms and garlic and cook over medium heat, stirring frequently, for 3–5 minutes, or until tender. Remove the skillet from the heat. Mix the bread crumbs, milk, and olive oil together in a large bowl, then stir in the ricotta, mushroom mixture, and 4 tablespoons of the Parmesan cheese. Season with salt and pepper.

4 Fill the cannelloni tubes with the mushroom mixture and place them in the dish. Brush with olive oil and sprinkle with the remaining Parmesan cheese, pine nuts, and almonds. Bake in a preheated oven, 375°F/190°C, for 25 minutes, or until golden.

cannelloni with spinach & ricotta

ingredients

SERVES 4

12 dried cannelloni tubes,
 3 inches/7.5 cm long
butter, for greasing

filling

5 oz/140 g cooked lean ham,
 chopped
5 oz/140 g frozen spinach,
 thawed and drained
4 oz/115 g/$\frac{1}{2}$ cup ricotta
 cheese
1 egg
3 tbsp freshly grated romano
 cheese
pinch of freshly grated nutmeg
salt and pepper

cheese sauce

2 tbsp unsalted butter
2 tbsp all-purpose flour
20 fl oz/625 ml/$2\frac{1}{2}$ cups
 hot milk
3 oz/85 g/$\frac{3}{4}$ cup freshly
 grated Gruyère cheese
salt and pepper

method

1 Bring a large pan of lightly salted water to a boil. Add the cannelloni tubes, return to a boil, and cook for 6–7 minutes, or until nearly tender. Drain and rinse under cold water. Spread out the tubes on a clean dish towel.

2 Process the ham, spinach, and ricotta in a food processor for a few seconds until combined. Add the egg and romano cheese and process again to a smooth paste. Transfer to a bowl and season with nutmeg, salt, and pepper.

3 Grease an ovenproof dish with butter. Spoon the filling into a pastry bag fitted with a $\frac{1}{2}$-inch/ 1-cm tip. Carefully pipe the filling into the cannelloni tubes and place in the dish.

4 To make the cheese sauce, melt the butter in a pan. Add the flour and cook over low heat, stirring constantly, for 1 minute. Gradually stir in the hot milk then bring to a boil, stirring constantly. Simmer over the lowest possible heat, stirring frequently, for 10 minutes until thickened and smooth. Remove the pan from the heat, stir in the Gruyère cheese, and season with salt and pepper.

5 Spoon the cheese sauce over the filled cannelloni. Cover the dish with foil and bake in a preheated oven, 350°F/180°C, for 20–25 minutes. Serve immediately.